This Book Belongs To:

_____

a woman who desires to know the mysteries of the kingdom.

MYSTERIES OF THE KINGDOM REVEALED

MYSTERIES OF THE KINGDOM REVEALED

A Study Of The Parables Of Jesus For Women

TERESA L. SKEPPLE

EDEN BOOK PRESS ● MORROW GEORGIA

EDEN BOOK PRESS
Morrow, Georgia, USA

Unless otherwise noted, Scripture taken are from the *New American Standard Bible*, © 1960, 1962, 1963, 1968, 1871, 1972, 1973, 1975, 1977, by The Lockman Foundation. Used by permission.

ISBN 978-0966056259
Suggested Subject Headings: Christian Living, Women, Bible Study, Parables, Gospels, Theology

© 2017
Teresa L. Skepple. All rights reserved. Printed in the United States of America.

Cover Design: Trina Alleyne
                    Joseph Banks

No part of this book may be reproduced without written permission, except for brief quotations in books and critical reviews.

This Bible study is gratefully dedicated

To

Him

"Who is able to do exceeding abundantly
beyond all that we ask or think,
according to the power that works within us."

ACKNOWLEDGMENTS

A special thanks to:

Dr. Opel Askew
Thank you for your tireless work in reading and editing each chapter. Your thoughts and suggestions have been so helpful to me in writing the Bible study. It has been said that some people come into your life and quickly go. Others stay a while and leave footprints on your heart and you are never the same. Thank you for the footprints you have left on my heart.

Charlotte Travis
You have been an inspiration and encouragement to me in writing this Bible study. Thank you for your love and commitment to the Lord and for faithfully teaching women here in the United States and abroad what it means to abide in Him! I am very blessed to call you my friend, my mentor and my spiritual sister in Christ.

Trina Alleyne
Thank you for helping me decide on a title and designing the front cover of the workbook. I am so grateful to the Lord for bringing you into my life and for the times we have studied the Scriptures together. Your love for the Lord and His Word is contagious!

Joseph Banks
Thank you for your professional and artistic expertise in finalizing both the front and back cover of the workbook. Your patience, precision and perfection are evident in the excellent work you do.

Patrick Perkins
Your encouraging words after reading the first lesson I wrote led to you being drafted for the next seven. Thank you for the biblical analysis and helpful suggestions you offered in each chapter.

Frank Pass
Thank you for your careful attention to the details and construction of each paragraph. Your editing expertise is unmatched. I am very grateful for you.

Roger W. F. Skepple
My wonderful husband whose biblical and scholarly wisdom, insight, and understanding has guided me every step of the way in writing this Bible study. My relationship with the Lord and my growth in the Lord would not be what it is today without you.

TABLE OF CONTENTS

Foreword
5

Introduction
7

The Sower And The Seed
Time Will Tell
15

The Rich Fool
Tomorrow Is Not Promised
45

The Unmerciful Servant
Forgiveness From The Heart
65

The Ten Virgins
Are You Ready To Meet The Bridegroom?
93

The Talents
Serving While You Wait
115

The Unjust Judge
Pray Until You Pray
137

The Prodigal Son
Lost And Found
157

The Pursuit Of Life
The Narrow Gate vs. The Wide Gate
181

Bibliography
207

Foreword

Despite our best efforts, human beings have a tendency to love secrets. The idea that we can know something that no one knows or very few people know is for most people too tantalizing to resist. Our problem with secrets is that we love to pass them on to others. The Bible refers to this activity as gossip. But gossip does not apply to God. God in fact both has secrets and has passed them on to us, with the expectation that we will pass them on to others. No where is this more clearly seen than in the biblical reality of Jesus' parables. Although one of the most well known aspects of Jesus' approach to instructing believers, the parables are also one of the most difficult aspects of Jesus' instruction to interpret. This is one of the reasons why I am so thankful for *Mysteries of the Kingdom Revealed: A Study of the Parables of Jesus for Women*.

This Bible study sets out to guide the believer through the process of understanding not only the select parables that it has chosen to study, but it lays out a pattern for any woman who would like to gain a fuller understanding of all the parables spoken by Jesus. It shows the importance of understanding the parables of Jesus in the day in which they were given. It demonstrates that understanding the individual parables demands a grasp of the biblical context in which they appeared. It leads the student to ask the right questions and make the proper applications of the lessons learned from these parables in their own lives. By carefully following the author's guidance any Christian woman will find herself blessed and encouraged in her pursuit of becoming the woman God wants her to be.

I know the author well, Teresa Skepple is my wife of thirty years. Teresa is a faithful communicator of God's Word and has embraced the pattern of the New Testament laid out for Christian woman with the gift of teaching, the pattern of teaching children and women. Finding resources written for women by women who embrace and defend these ideals is a difficult task in deed, but in this resource you have found one. Any women's Bible Study, Sunday School Class, or Small Group will benefit from this excellent resource.

Mysteries of the Kingdom Revealed will help you live a life that honors the salvation you have experienced. Paul told the Colossians, "For He delivered us from the domain of darkness, and transferred us to the kingdom of His beloved Son, in whom we have redemption, the forgiveness of sins" (Col. 1:13-14). Kingdom living is Christian living and through an understanding of the parables of Jesus, you will solidify your understanding of what such a life looks like. Enjoy.

Roger W. F. Skepple, Senior Pastor
Berean Bible Baptist Church

MYSTERIES OF THE KINGDOM REVEALED

A Study Of The Parables Of Jesus For Women
"He Who Has Ears, Let Him Hear"
Matthew 13:9

INTRODUCTION

"The Bible is one story,
that unfolds in one book, by one author,
about one subject...
a story that moves from promise to fulfillment."
– Alistair Begg

I love a good story. Well told stories have a way of grabbing your attention and drawing you in to the very heart and soul of the message. Whether reading a good book or watching an epic motion picture you can become so captivated by the events in the story that you are no longer a mere listener but a willing participant. You may even begin to anticipate how the story will end. You probably know of people who skip ahead and take a peek at the last chapter of a book because they cannot wait to find out what happens in the end. Endings to stories can be very powerful. They also tend to grab your attention and ignite certain emotions, especially when there is an unexpected ending.

Jesus was a Master Storyteller. I have often tried to imagine what it would have been like to be sitting with a group of people or walking through the vineyards or along the shores of the Sea of Galilee, with Jesus just a few feet ahead telling one of His stories. Thankfully, many of them have been recorded for us in the Bible to read again and again.

However, the stories Jesus told were not just stories. Jesus said,

"I came that they may have life and have it abundantly."
John 10:10

Jesus' stories were skillfully formed and perfectly suited to communicate life-changing truth to the listener of His time and to us today. Jesus' stories are eternal truths that teach and instruct in the most effective way about the very life that He came to give. The life He came to give is available to all. It is available to all who are weary and heavy-laden. It is available to all who come to Him and take His yoke upon themselves and learn from Him.

However, there is one caveat...you must have "ears to hear." Sometimes Jesus added on to the end of His stories the phrase "he who has ears, let him hear." But what does that mean? Jesus explained the phrase to His disciples when He said,

> **"To you it has been granted to know the mysteries**
> **of the kingdom of heaven, But to them it has not been granted."**
> **Matthew 13:11**

With that statement, Jesus also disclosed the fact that there are only two kinds of people in the world. Although we come in different shapes, sizes, colors, personalities, backgrounds, nationalities, and from all walks of life, the Bible speaks of only two kinds of people and they are described in several ways:

- Those to whom it has been granted to know the mysteries of the Kingdom of Heaven and those to whom it has not been granted (Matthew 13:11).

- Those who bear good fruit and those who bear bad fruit (Matthew 7:16-20).

- Those who build on the rock and those who build on the sand (Matthew 7:24-27).

- Those who enter through the narrow gate and those who enter through the wide gate (Matthew 7:13-14).

- Those who store up treasures in heaven and those who store up treasures on earth (Matthew 6:19-21).

- Those who seek first His Kingdom and righteousness and those who eagerly seek the things of the world (Matthew 6:32-33).

- Those who have ears to hear and those who do not have ears to hear (Matthew 13:9).

Notice Jesus continued His explanation when He said,

> **"For whoever has, to him more shall be given, and he will have an abundance;**
> **But whoever does not have, even what he has shall be taken away from him.**
> **Therefore I speak to them in parables; because while seeing they do not see,**
> **And while hearing they do not hear, nor do they understand.**
> **In their case the prophecy of Isaiah is being fulfilled, which says,**
> **'You will keep on hearing, but will not understand;**
> **You will keep on seeing, but will not perceive;**
> **For the heart of this people has become dull,**
> **With their ears they scarcely hear,**
> **And they have closed their eyes,**
> **Otherwise they would see with their eyes,**
> **Hear with their ears,**
> **And understand with their heart and return,**
> **And I would heal them.'**
> **But blessed are your eyes, because they see;**
> **And your ears, because they hear.**
> **For truly I say to you that many prophets and righteous men**
> **desired to see what you see, and did not see it,**
> **And to hear what you hear, and did not hear it."**
> **Matthew 13:12-17**

Jesus decided to speak in parables because of the crowds of people following Him. They were a mixed group and some were superficial listeners.

There were people in the crowd who just wanted to see the next miracle Jesus performed. There were people who wanted to be close enough to get whatever He offered to give. There were those who according to Matthew 22:15 "plotted together how they might trap Him in what He said," we know them as the Pharisees and religious leaders.

However, there were also genuine followers, people who had a "hunger and thirst for righteousness," people to whom it was granted to know the mysteries of the kingdom of heaven.

Therefore, Jesus had a three-fold purpose for speaking in parables.

1. To reveal truth to His genuine followers
2. To conceal truth from His enemies and superficial listeners
3. To fulfill prophecy (Isaiah 6:9-10)

Mysteries of the Kingdom Revealed

WHAT IS A PARABLE

The word "parable" comes from the Greek word παραβολη (parabolee). In the Greek, "para" means beside or alongside, and "ballo" means to cast or throw. A parable has also been defined as a teaching aid cast alongside the truth being taught. It is the idea of comparing two realities that mirror each other. In it's simplest form, a parable is an earthly story that conveys a spiritual truth.[1]

Although Jesus used parables in much of His teaching ministry, He was not the first one to speak in a parable. In fact, parables were also used in the Old Testament, and a very familiar one is found in II Samuel 12:1-7a.

You remember the horrible story of David committing adultery with Bathsheba and in an attempt to cover his sin, had her husband Uriah killed in battle. After marrying Bathsheba, a whole year went by before God sent the Prophet Nathan to pay David a visit. When Nathan arrived, he told David a parable about a rich man stealing from a poor man. As David listened he became more and more enraged until in anger he said, "Surely as the Lord lives, the man that has done this deserves to die"...and Nathan immediately responded with the words, "You, are the man."

Then David understood the parable was about him and he confessed his sin to Nathan. Psalm 51 records David's prayer of confession and pleading for forgiveness from the Lord.

"Some sections of the Bible give us grand theology.
Some move us to grateful responses to God.
The parables ask us if there has been any real difference in our lives."
– James Montgomery Boice

---

[1] Verlyn D, Verbrugge *The NIV Theological Dictionary of New Testament Words,* (Zondervan Publishing House, Grand Rapids MI, 2000), 958.

MYSTERIES OF THE KINGDOM REVEALED

A STUDY OF THE PARABLES OF JESUS FOR WOMEN
"He Who Has Ears, Let Him Hear"
Matthew 13:9

PURPOSE

Mysteries Of The Kingdom Revealed is a Bible study for women that came about out of a desire for an in depth study of the parables Jesus taught. It is the goal of this Bible study that women will see themselves spiritually and examine their own heart in light of the "mysteries of the Kingdom" revealed.

In the parables, we are uniquely confronted with fundamental truths about God, about ourselves and about how to live and relate to others in a fallen world. As we submit ourselves to the truths Jesus taught, God uses them to alter and shape our Christian walk resulting in greater obedience to His Word. Jesus said, "If you know these things, <u>blessed</u> are you if you do them" (John 13:17).

Many times we read the parables and recognize the meaning but rarely contemplate the implications of the message for our own life personally. One of the reasons Jesus often ended His parables with the phrase, "He who has ears to hear, let him hear," is because He was challenging His audience to consider their ways and humbly submit in obedience to His Word. I want you to view each lesson as an opportunity to be challenged by the Lord Jesus Christ. He not only wants you to know His Word but to align your life in obedience to His Word!

The Bible study was designed to be used in a group setting but can be studied individually. However one of the benefits of studying with a group of ladies is the encouragement you will receive and the tremendous enrichment you will gain as others share what God has taught them from the lesson.

PRESENTATION

Mysteries of the Kingdom Revealed contains eight parables and was written for a ladies Sunday school class. Within each chapter you will discover additional topics that can be pursued for further enrichment. Each chapter also contains numerous questions designed to promote application of the lesson. To get the most out of the Bible study do not attempt to complete a parable in a one hour segment of time. If you are leading a small group or facilitating a class, consider reviewing each chapter beforehand and identifying the additional topics you would like to pursue for further enrichment. Next determine how much time you will need to adequately teach the lesson including any additional topics. Lastly, set your schedule. You will notice some parables are longer than others however, each lesson can be adapted to the time frame of your choosing.

Each lesson contains:

- The Scripture passage that introduces the parable. Although some parables appear in all three of the Synopic gospels (Matthew, Mark, Luke), the passage referenced will be the main passage used in the lesson. Unless otherwise noted, all Scripture passages are from the New American Standard Version.

- A summary containing the theme of the parable, Scripture reference, the occasion in which the parable was taught, a brief overview of the parable and a Psalm to help prepare your heart to receive God's Word.

- Questions for both group discussion and personal reflection. Each question will enrich your understanding of the lesson and lead you to greater obedience to the Lord.

- A prayer from "The Valley Of Vision," A Collection Of Puritan Prayers and Devotions.

- Lined paper for additional notes.

PREPARATION

As with any Bible study, always <u>begin with prayer</u>. Ask the Lord to open your heart and prepare you to receive from Him. I like the way the Psalmist said it:

> **"Teach me, O Lord, the way of Your statutes,**
> **And I shall observe it to the end.**
> **Give me understanding,**
> **That I may observe Your law and keep it with all my heart.**
> **Make me walk in the path of Your commandments,**
> **For I delight in it.**
> **Incline my heart to Your testimonies and not to dishonest gain."**
> **Psalm 119:33-36**

The question was asked: Do you believe God talks to you? The answer is yes! God graciously speaks to each of us <u>through His Word</u>.

When I study the Word, it is as if I am getting one-on-one teaching, encouragement and instruction by none other than God Himself. He enables me to see things that I cannot see apart from Him and to understand things I cannot understand apart from Him. I love hearing God speak through the study of His Word!

I am excited and thankful to the Lord for this Bible study. I look forward to studying with you and hearing from you how the Lord used it in your life. Welcome and get ready to have the mysteries of the kingdom revealed to you personally!

– Teresa

TO THE PRAISE AND GLORY OF HIS GREAT NAME!

SPEAK O LORD,

"As we come to You To receive the food of Your Holy Word.

Take Your truth, plant it deep in us; Shape and fashion us in Your likeness,

That the light of Christ might be seen today

In our acts of love and our deeds of faith.

Speak, O Lord, and fulfill in us all Your purposes for Your glory.

Teach us, Lord, full obedience, holy reverence, true humility;

Test our thoughts and our attitudes

In the radiance of Your purity.

Cause our faith to rise; cause our eyes to see

Your majestic love and authority.

Words of pow'r that can never fail—

Let their truth prevail over unbelief.

Speak, O Lord, and renew our minds;

Help us grasp the heights of Your plans for us—

Truths unchanged from the dawn of time

That will echo down through eternity.

And by grace we'll stand on Your promises,

And by faith we'll walk as You walk with us.

Speak, O Lord, till Your church is built

And the earth is filled with Your glory."

– Keith Getty & Stuart Townend

THE SOWER AND THE SEED

THE SOWER AND THE SEED

MARK 4:1-20

"He began to teach again by the sea. And such a very large crowd gathered to Him that He got into a boat in the sea and sat down; and the whole crowd was by the sea on the land. And He was teaching them many things in parables, and was saying to them in His teaching, 'Listen to this! Behold, the sower went out to sow; as he was sowing, some seed fell beside the road, and the birds came and ate it up. Other seed fell on the rocky ground where it did not have much soil; and immediately it sprang up because it had no depth of soil. And after the sun had risen, it was scorched; and because it had no root, it withered away. Other seed fell among the thorns, and the thorns came up and choked it, and it yielded no crop. Other seeds fell into the good soil, and as they grew up and increased, they yielded a crop and produced thirty, sixty, and a hundredfold.' And He was saying, 'He who has ears to hear, let him hear.'

As soon as He was alone, His followers, along with the twelve, began asking Him about the parables. And He was saying to them, 'To you has been given the mysteries of the kingdom of God, but those who are outside get everything in parables, so that while seeing, they may see and not perceive, and while hearing, they may hear and not understand, otherwise they might return and be forgiven.'

EXPLANATION

And He said to them, 'Do you not understand this parable? How will you understand all the parables? The sower sows the word. These are the ones who are beside the road where the word is sown; and when they hear, immediately Satan comes and takes away the word which has been sown in them. In a similar way these are the ones on whom seed was sown on the rocky places, who, when they hear the word, immediately receive it with joy; and they have no firm root in themselves, but are only temporary; then, when affliction or persecution arises because of the word, immediately they fall away. And others are the ones on whom seed was sown among the thorns; these are the ones who have heard the word, but the worries of the world, and the deceitfulness of riches, and the desires for other things enter in and choke the word, and it becomes unfruitful. And those are the ones on whom seed was sown on the good soil; and they hear the word and accept it and bear fruit, thirty, sixty, and a hundredfold.'"

THE SOWER AND THE SEED
Time Will Tell

Theme: Genuine Faith Produces Genuine Fruit

Scripture: Mark 4:1-20

Occasion: Jesus was teaching by the Sea of Galilee, but after a large crowd of people converged upon Him, He got into a boat in the sea and continued teaching from there. Jesus started His parabolic ministry after being confronted by the Pharisees and accused of casting out demons by Beelzebul "the ruler of the demons" (Matthew 12:24).

Overview: The Parable of the Sower is the very first parable Jesus taught. Therefore, it is important in that it sets the tone as well as the interpretive structure of all the rest of His parables. Before Jesus gave the meaning of the parable He asked a question. He said, "Do you not understand this parable? How will you understand all the parables" (Mark 4:13)? The key to understanding this parable and all other parables of Jesus has to do with the way you hear. The word "hear" or "listen" appears thirteen times in Mark 4. In the parable, Jesus identifies four different types of soil and how each responded to the seed that fell upon it. He then illustrates how each of the four soils are representative of the hearts of man in response to the preached Word of God.

Heart Preparation: "Teach me to do Your will, for You are my God; let Your good Spirit lead me on level ground" (Psalm 143:10).

THE SOWER AND THE SEED
Time Will Tell

Growing up in the church I learned at a young age that not everyone who attends church and ministers in the church, remains with the church. Unfortunately, sometimes people leave. Perhaps some may join another church. Others continue the pattern of moving from one church to another or leave church permanently.

The excuses and reasons people state for leaving the church are as varied as the people themselves. It's no surprise that some of the most common reasons involve people and poor or broken relationships. Too much drama, too many cliques, and being hurt by someone are almost always at the top of any list of reasons. One blogger stated that

> "People leave church when they don't find Jesus.
> With the exception of religious conservatives,
> everyone longed to be around Jesus and went to
> great lengths and great risk to spend time with him."[1]

That's a nice thought, however, the Bible presents a different view of how some people responded to Jesus. The Bible demonstrates that Jesus had a way of saying things that divided people and caused controversy, resulting in people not wanting to be around Him. On one occasion Jesus said,

> **"Do you suppose that I came to grant peace on earth?**
> **I tell you, no, but rather division;**
> **For from now on five members in one household will be divided,**
> **Three against two and two against three.**
> **They will be divided father against son and son against father,**
> **Mother against daughter and daughter against mother,**
> **Mother-in-law against daughter-in-law**
> **And daughter-in-law against mother-in-law."**
> **Luke 12:51-53**

In John 6 the large crowd of followers heard Jesus say,

> **"Truly, truly I say to you,**
> **Unless you eat the flesh of the Son of Man and drink His blood,**
> **You have no life in yourselves."**
> **John 6:53**

---

[1] Dr Benjamin L. Corey. "*10 Reasons Why People Leave Church*" http://www.patheos.com/blogs/formerlyfundie/*10-reasons-why-people-leave-church* (accessed January 2017).

That statement to be expected, resulted in the fact that "many of His disciples withdrew and were not walking with Him anymore" (John 6:66).

Why did they leave? Why did they lose interest in Jesus and what He was teaching? The Parable of the Sower helps us understand why people respond to Jesus and His Word the way they do.

1. Read **Mark 4:1-20** and jot down any thoughts that come to mind.

___

Before we study the parable, let's first talk about the Sovereignty of God. So much of the Parable of the Sower points to it.

- Who determined those who would have ears to hear and those who would not?
- Who determined those who would be given the mystery of the Kingdom and those who would "get everything in parables?"
- Who provided the seed for the Sower to sow?
- Who caused the seed to fall on "good" soil?
- Who made the soil good?
- Who caused the good soil to produce fruit in various amounts?

The answers to these questions are all the same, our Sovereign God!

One of the many attributes of God is that He is Sovereign. You don't have to read any further than the first verse of the Bible to know this about God.

> **"In the beginning <u>God</u> created the heavens and the earth."**
> **Genesis 1:1**

When we say God is Sovereign, it refers to His Lordship. It means to reign and rule over all. Listen to the way God describes Himself in Isaiah:

> **"Remember the former things long past,**
> **For I am God and there is no other;**
> **I am God and there is no one like Me,**
> **Declaring the end from the beginning,**

> **And from ancient times things which have
> not been done, saying:
> 'My purpose will be established,
> And I will accomplish all My good pleasure.'"
> Isaiah 46:9-10**

God set forth and established all events of human history. He orders, controls, and owns everything in the heavens and on the earth. God controls even the evil that takes place in the world. Notice how God handled the perilous situation in the garden after Adam and Eve sinned against Him.

> **"'Behold the man has become like one of Us
> knowing good and evil; And now, he might stretch out his hand,
> and take also from the tree of life, And eat and live forever.'
> Therefore the Lord God sent him out from the garden of Eden,
> to cultivate the ground from which he was taken.
> So He drove the man out, and at the east of the garden of Eden
> He stationed the cherubim and the flaming sword
> which turned every direction to guard the way to the Tree of Life."
> Genesis 3:22-24**

If God had not intervened and removed Adam and Eve from the garden, they would have eaten from the Tree of Life and been sealed in their sinful state. Mankind would have been unredeemable and eternally separated from God. God sovereignly intervened limiting the evil outcome.

God's sovereign control also means that as His daughters, we can be confident that whatever happens to us personally, was allowed by God. We can be confident knowing that times of great joy and celebration as well as times of great sorrow and heartache, are under the sovereignty of God. Even sinful acts we have or will commit, wrong choices and bad decisions, are all a part of His plan and therefore under His Sovereign control. However, God's sovereignty must never become an excuse for unfaithfulness on our part.

God's sovereign control means that He has determined everything pertaining to you and your life, beforehand. God has planned every day of your life and in time, providentially causes it to unfold <u>precisely</u> as He planned.

2. Look up the following verses. Jot down a sentence or two about God's Sovereignty.

   A. **Daniel 4:35**

   B. **Psalm 115:3**

   C. **II Chronicles 20:6**

   D. **Isaiah 43:13**

   E. **Luke 1:37**

   F. **Colossians 1:17**

The Sower and the Seed

G. **Revelation 21:6**

_____
_____
_____
_____

Let's return to the Parable of the Sower in Mark 4.

> **"He began to teach again by the sea.**
> **And such a very large crowd gathered**
> **to Him that He got into a boat in the sea and sat down;**
> **and the whole crowd was by the sea on the land."**
> **Mark 4:1**

Jesus garnered popularity very early in His ministry. After He was baptized, He endured forty days and forty nights of satanic temptation and once that ended, He began selecting the twelve disciples and launched His ministry.

3. According to **Matthew 4:23-24,** what contributed to the popularity of Jesus?

_____
_____
_____
_____

Matthew recorded that "large crowds followed Him from Galilee and the Decapolis and Jerusalem and Judea and from beyond the Jordan" (Matthew 4:25). People had heard about Him performing miracles, healing diseases, giving sight to the blind and drastically changing lives. Naturally, people were intrigued and wanted to get close to Him and perhaps be the recipient of one of His miracles. When Jesus saw the large crowd He "got into a boat in the sea and sat down and the whole crowd was by the sea on the land" (Mark 4:1).

They listened to His story about a sower and what happened when the seed fell on the soil, but were no doubt baffled by the meaning of it all. Most of the people in the crowd were farmers themselves and quite aware of the results of planting seeds in various types of soil. "What is the point?" was probably on the mind of many of the people that day, but when Jesus concluded His story with an unusual statement, they were even more confused.

Mysteries of the Kingdom Revealed

4. Read **Mark 4:9** again and write it on the lines below.

_____
_____
_____
_____

Verse 9 is the most important verse in the parable. Verse 9 directs your attention to the matter of hearing. Jesus was not talking about hearing with your physical ears, but a different kind of hearing which will become more apparent as we study the parable. If you are a believer, the way you hear the Word of God and what you do with what you hear either authenticates your relationship with the Lord or invalidates it.

According to James, believers are to be doers of the Word and not "merely hearers only who delude themselves" (James 1:22). Jesus said, "My sheep *hear* My voice, and I know them, and they follow Me" (John 10:27).

Your goal, your purpose and desire as a believer is to follow through in obedience to what you have heard.

The statement Jesus made in Mark 4:9 most likely contributed to the crowd's response to Him. While they may have been interested in knowing about the kingdom, His teaching on seeds and soil made no sense to them. According to Mark 4:10 when Jesus had finished teaching for the day, most of the crowd left and only "His followers along with the twelve" remained. Notice what Jesus said to those who remained:

> **"To you has been given to know the mysteries of the Kingdom of God**
> **But those who are outside get everything in parables.**
> **So that while seeing they may see and not perceive,**
> **And while hearing, they may hear and not understand,**
> **Otherwise they might return and be forgiven."**
> **Mark 4:11-12**

5. How does it make you feel knowing that you are among those granted to know the "mysteries of the kingdom?"

_____
_____
_____
_____
_____

The Sower and the Seed

The Greek word μυστήριον *(musterion)* translated "mystery" does not mean something unknowable. Rather, it is what can only be known through revelation, i.e. because God reveals it.[2] When the Bible mentions "mystery," it doesn't keep the secret, it reveals it.

A portion of Jesus' statement in Mark 4:11-12 was a quote taken from Isaiah. Isaiah lived approximately 700 years prior to the birth of Christ and was commissioned by God to warn the people of his day of impending judgment.

6. Read **Isaiah 6:9-10**. What did God tell Isaiah to say to the people?

_____
_____
_____
_____
_____

The statement by God leveled against the people in Isaiah's day was judgment brought on due to their hardened hearts.

Let's examine more closely exactly what they did to incur the judgment of God.

7. According to **Isaiah 1:2-4**, what were the indictments God declared against the Children of Israel?

_____
_____
_____
_____
_____

8. According to **Isaiah 3:8-9,** in what ways did the Children of Israel bring evil upon themselves?

_____
_____
_____
_____
_____

---

[2]http://biblehub.com/greek/3466.htm. *Strong's Exhaustive Concordance*, NASB Translation.

Mysteries of the Kingdom Revealed

9. According to **Isaiah 5:1-2**, what did God do for the Children of Israel and what did He receive from them in return?

___

10. According to **Isaiah 5:5-6**, how did God respond after receiving worthless fruit?

___

11. Read **Isaiah 5:8-25** for further understanding of the hard-heartedness of the Children of Israel. Write any thoughts or observations below.

___

God did everything necessary for His people to bear good fruit, grow spiritually, and glorify Him. He gave them every advantage, even providing a hedge of protection around them. Though God expected good fruit, what was produced was "worthless" (evil) fruit. Because of their rebellious ways, God instituted a judicial hardening. In His judgment God was essentially saying, "Since you continue to demonstrate willful disobedience and blatant disregard for Me, from now on you will be unable to hear, understand and consequently obey what I say."

Notice again what is said in Isaiah:

> "**Render the hearts of this people insensitive,**
> **Their ears dull, And their eyes dim,**
> **Otherwise they might see with their eyes,**
> **Hear with their ears, Understand with their hearts,**
> **And return and be healed."**
> **Isaiah 6:10**

The word "insensitive" means unreceptive. They had closed their mind towards God. As a result, God hardened their hearts so that while hearing they would not perceive and while seeing they would not understand what they saw.

Throughout the ministry of Christ, the religious leaders and Pharisees acted in similar ways. Notice how they responded after observing the healing of a demon possessed man.

> **"As they were going out, a mute, demon possessed man was brought to Him.
> After the demon was cast out, the mute man spoke
> and the crowds were amazed, and were saying,
> 'Nothing like this has ever been seen in Israel.' But the Pharisees were saying,
> 'He casts out the demons by the ruler of the demons.'"
> Matthew 9:32-34**

Jesus performed miracle after miracle. He fed well over 5000 people with two fish and five loaves of bread. He healed the sick and enabled the blind to see and the lame to walk. Yet, according to John, the people asked Jesus:

> **"What then do You do for a sign so that we may *see* and believe You?
> What work do You perform?"
> John 6:30**

Just as Isaiah prophesied, the people would keep on listening but not perceive, and they would keep on looking but not understand. The people had turned from the Word of the Lord in Isaiah's day and the same was occurring in the days of Jesus. Hard-heartedness and disbelief resulted in them not being able to recognize Jesus for who He is.

Simon Peter recognized Jesus and his confession of faith was recorded by John. Read **John 6:68-69** and write it on the lines below.

_____
_____
_____
_____
_____
_____

> **"To you has been given the mystery of the kingdom of God,**
> **But those who are outside get everything in parables.**
> **So that while seeing, they may see and not perceive,**
> **And while hearing they may hear and not understand,**
> **Otherwise they might return and be forgiven."**
> **Mark 4:11-12**

As stated earlier, Jesus had a three-fold purpose for speaking in parables.

1. To reveal truth to His genuine followers (Those to whom it was granted)
2. To conceal truth from His enemies and superficial listeners (The "outsiders")
3. To fulfill the prophecy of Isaiah (Isaiah 6:9-10)

It's not too difficult to understand that rebellion, rejection, and hard-heartedness prevent people from hearing and understanding the mysteries of the Kingdom. Jesus refers to them as "outsiders," who are judged by God in that the truth is concealed from them.

What is difficult to understand are the "outsiders" who do not look like "outsiders" and do not act like "outsiders" but instead have an outward appearance of righteousness and obedience to the Word. Paul in his ministry described that kind of person as "holding to a form of godliness..." (2 Timothy 3:5).

Through the Parable of the Sower, Jesus not only identified the "outsiders" but also the "genuine followers" by illustrating how four different types of soil responded to the seed that fell upon it.

> **"The sower sows the Word."**
> **Mark 4:14**

The first thing Jesus taught was that the seed represented the Word of God. Just as a sower in His day would go out and sow seeds for the purpose of producing fruit, so the Word of God was to be sown with a similar expectation. Jesus was communicating to His listeners that the Word of God must be sown. Notice, Jesus does not say anything else about the sower. He only mentioned what the sower did because the sower represents any born again believer.

As believers, we are all sowers. We are expected by God to sow His Word. As a mother, I am responsible to sow the Word of God in my children and it must start when they are very young. I am responsible to "train up a child in the way he should go...."
(Proverbs 22:6); that means sowing the Word.

The Sower and the Seed

The workplace, the neighborhood, family and friends all provide opportunities to sow the Word of God into the life of another.

12. What do you learn from the following Scriptures about sowing the Word? Write your thoughts on the lines below.

A. **Matthew 28:18-20**

B. **Romans 10:14-17**

C. **Acts 8:29-35**

13. In the parable we know that the seed represents the Word of God. According to **Luke 8:11-12**, what does the soil represent?

Knowing what the soil represents is critical in understanding the point of the parable. Because of the reality of counterfeit faith, Jesus wanted His disciples to recognize that the way people respond to Him was not because of a head problem but a heart problem.

Although we are confronted with numerous troubles and temptations from the world and the enemy of our soul, our greatest problem comes from within. The condition of our heart greatly impacts not only our physical life but more importantly, our eternal life. Authentic faith comes about only through the power and work of God in a person's heart.

The Pharisees and religious leaders of Jesus' day got it all wrong. Their focus was on maintaining an outward appearance of righteousness. Jesus rebuked them for their sinful ways when He said,

> **"Woe to you, scribes and Pharisees, hypocrites!**
> **For you clean the outside of the cup and of the dish,**
> **But inside they are full of robbery and self-indulgence.**
> **You blind Pharisee, first clean the inside of the cup and of the dish,**
> **So that the outside of it may become clean also.**
> **Woe to you, scribes and Pharisees, hypocrites!**
> **For you are like whitewashed tombs which on the outside appear beautiful,**
> **But inside they are full of dead men's bones and all uncleanness.**
> **So you, too, outwardly appear righteous to men,**
> **But inwardly you are full of hypocrisy and lawlessness."**
> **Matthew 23:25-28**

In the explanation of The Parable of the Sower, Jesus stated the reason why each of the four soils responded differently to the seed. As we study the explanation, you must ask yourself:
- Which soil represents my heart?
- Which soil reflects my experience in life?
- Which soil represents my response when I hear the Word of God?

> **"These are the ones who are beside the road where the word is sown;**
> **And when they hear, immediately Satan comes**
> **And takes away the word which has been sown in them."**
> **Mark 4:15**

Just as Isaiah prophesied, this is the person whose eyes are dim and ears are dull. They hear the Word, but their hearing does not result in obedience to the Lord. What is shocking about this individual is that the Word was sown in them and yet Satan was able to take it away. How can that happen? How can the Word of God be sown into an individual and Satan take it away from them?

Satan is compared to the birds mentioned in verse four. Just as they converged upon the soil and quickly ate the seeds, so Satan comes and takes away the Word immediately as the hearer hears it. The Word has no effect upon this person's life because it has no entrance into their heart. Their heart is hardened and therefore not opened to the Word of the Lord.

14. Look up the verses on the following page and write down what you learn about the heart.

A. **Jeremiah 7:24**

B. **Jeremiah 17:9-10**

C. **Proverbs 4:23**

D. **Ezekiel 33:30-32**

E. **Ezekiel 36:26**

F. **Hebrews 3:15**

Mysteries of the Kingdom Revealed

G. **Proverbs 2:2**

_____
_____
_____
_____
_____

H. **Proverbs 23:12**

_____
_____
_____
_____
_____

Although, in Scripture ears are the pathway to the heart, it does not mean that the heart receives what the ears transport. Hearts that are deceptive, not inclined to the Word, hardened, or disobedient provide access to an enemy who comes only to "steal, kill and destroy" (John 10:10). As to the Word being taken away after being "sown in them," I think the author of Hebrews offers the best explanation of how that happens.

15. Read **Hebrews 6:1-8** and complete the chart below.

The Word "Sown-In" the Believer (v. 1-3)	Resulting in... (v. 7)
vs. 1 – Received the elementary truths about Christ vs. 2 – Pressed on to maturity vs. 3 – Did not lay a foundation again	
The Word "Sown-In" the Unbeliever (v. 4-6)	Resulting in... (v. 8)
vs. 4 – Was enlightened vs. 4 – Tasted the heavenly gift vs. 4 – Was made partaker of the Holy Spirit vs. 5 – Tasted the good Word of God vs. 6 – Fell away	

The soil Jesus referred to as "beside the road" represented the person whose heart was closed. It is evidenced by the fact that they are completely unphased and unaffected by the Word. Even what was sown in them was taken away. Therefore, they remained unchanged and there was no lingering presence of God's Word in them.

> **"In a similar way these are the ones on whom seed was sown on the rocky places,**
> **Who, when they hear the Word, immediately receive it with joy;**
> **And they have no firm root in themselves, but are only temporary;**
> **Then, when affliction or persecution arises because of the Word,**
> **Immediately they fall away."**
> **Mark 4:16-17**

The seed sown on the rocky places represented the person whose hearing was superficial. They heard and were attentive to the Word. Perhaps their heart was filled with thoughts of experiencing a new life and a new start and they wanted it. Their joy and excitement over the Word compelled them to respond with no hesitation and no delay.

However, Jesus identified a major flaw in the person which no amount of enthusiasm or excitement could overcome. Having "no firm root in themselves" resulted in a temporary outcome. The quick response to the Word was short-lived. Not only was the response short-lived, but the attitude that led to the quick response was short-lived. Something occurred in this person's life that unmasked their true colors.

16. What two problems occurred that exposed this person's true colors?

    _____

Just as quickly as the superficial hearer responded to the Word, he abandoned the Word when faced with hardship and unpleasant circumstances. Although the hearer responded with joy, it was not the joy of the Lord, nor was it the joy that comes from an authentic relationship with the Lord.

In fact, the joy of the genuine believer exults "in our tribulations, knowing that tribulation brings about perseverance; and perseverance, proven character and proven character hope and hope does not disappoint because the love of God has been poured out within our hearts through the Holy Spirit who was given to us" (Romans 5:3-5).

17. Affliction, persecution, trials and temptation can absolutely create an environment for believers to respond sinfully. What do the following Scriptures tell us about God's expectation when His children are experiencing difficult circumstances?

Ecclesiastes 7:14 _____

Psalm 27:13-14 _____

Mysteries of the Kingdom Revealed

Psalm 42:11 _____

John 16:33 _____

Romans 12:12 _____

Ephesians 6:13 _____

James 1:2 _____

I Peter 4:12-13 _____

> "And others are the ones on whom seed was sown among the thorns;
> These are the ones who have heard the word,
> But the worries of the world, and the deceitfulness of riches,
> And the desires for other things enter in and choke the word,
> And it becomes unfruitful."
> **Mark 4:18-19**

The seed sown among thorns represents the person who is distracted. This person has a lot going on but not in a good way. Three things Jesus stated defined this person: "worries of the world, deceitfulness of riches and desire for other things" (Mark. 4:19).

Because all three categories are connected to each other, all three can co-exist in the person. For example, this person's desire for other things has no problem finding a place in a heart filled with worldly worries and the deceitfulness of riches because it provides "good soil" to thrive. The hearing and receiving of the Word of God does nothing to alter this person's attention and focus. Therefore, the Word is choked, resulting in unfruitfulness.

There are numerous illustrations of people in Scripture whose attention and focus on riches, desire for other things, and worldly worries choked the Word of God. One such individual was Simon the Magician.

18. Read **Acts 8:4-24** and jot down what stands out to you.

_____
_____
_____
_____

Chapter 8 begins with Saul before his conversion, rejoicing over the death of Stephen who had been murdered by members of the Sanhedrin. To celebrate, Saul began devastating the church by taking the people of God captive and putting them in prison.

Phillip the Evangelist was one of the many who were scattered due to Saul's persecution of the church. Phillip entered the city of Samaria and began "proclaiming Christ to them" (Acts 8:5). Simon the Magician was "practicing magic in the city and astonishing the people of Samaria, claiming to be someone great" (Acts 8:9). Whatever he was doing was so convincing that people were amazed to the point that they thought he had the very power of God (Acts 8:10). When Phillip arrived proclaiming the gospel of Jesus Christ, a large number of people received Christ and were baptized, including Simon the Magician.

It would appear that Simon had put away his magic tricks and became a genuine follower of Jesus. However, when Peter and John joined Phillip in Samaria, Simon's true identity was unveiled.

19. What do you see from the life of Simon that resembles the thorny soil Jesus described in the parable?

_____
_____
_____
_____
_____

What a tragedy that people can be taught the Word of God, abandon their past life, associate with the people of God and yet remain unconverted.

Simon is an example of the fact that hearing and receiving the Word does not necessarily lead to conversion. Getting baptized, continuing on with Phillip and being amazed as he observed the signs and great miracles could not overrule the fact that Simon was bitter and in the bondage of iniquity. His preoccupation and desire for power drove him to offer money in exchange for authority granted only by God (Acts 8:18-19).

The tragedy of all tragedies happened when Peter's stern rebuke went unheeded. Instead of repenting of his sin, Simon told Peter to, "pray to the Lord for me yourselves, so that nothing of what you have said may come upon me" (Acts 8:24). Clearly, he did not know the Lord.

**"And those are the ones on whom seed was sown on the good soil;
And they hear the Word and accept it and bear fruit,**

Thirty, sixty, and a hundredfold."
Mark 4:20

Finally, some good news! After three non-productive results, the last soil brought forth fruit.

Jesus explained that the seed sown on the "good soil" represented the person who hears the Word and accepts it and bears fruit. The difference between the last soil and the other three is obvious and vast. Not only was fruit produced from the last soil, but it was produced in varying amounts.

In Jesus' explanation, we see that just like the other three illustrations, this person heard the Word. However, something occurred in the hearing of the Word that was manifested in the fact that fruit was produced. The Word did something in the last person that the other three did not experience. Let's review the condition of the soil.

20. On the lines provided write a sentence or two summarizing each soil and how it responded to the seed.

The first soil: _____

The second soil: _____

The third soil: _____

The fourth soil: _____

The sower went out to sow seeds, but it wasn't until seed fell on the last soil, the "good" soil, that fruit was produced. Producing fruit was the sum total of what the sower expected and hoped for.

Fruit was what Jesus wanted His followers and disciples to understand about the parable but also about the Christian life. Fruit is what Jesus wants you and me to understand about the parable and the Christian life.

The reason Jesus had more to say about the second and third persons, represented by the rocky and thorny soils, had to do with fruit. Remember Jesus defined the second person as having "no firm root in themselves" (Mark 4:17) which resulted in a temporary outcome. Although the person appeared to manifest life, in time they fell away. Affliction and persecution rendered them fruitless. The third person also appeared to manifest life but, in time, that which filled their heart (worries, deceitful riches and worldly desires) choked the Word and it became unfruitful.

Bearing fruit is one way of having assurance of salvation, and I strongly believe it is so vitally important that we understand the critical nature of fruit-bearing in our life. Without fruit, there is no life.

In the Sermon on the Mount, Jesus warned His followers and disciples about false prophets. He warned them about those who practiced their righteousness before men. He warned them about those who appeared to be genuine but were counterfeit. Twice He stated, "You will know them by their fruits" (Matthew 7:16, 20). Fruit-bearing was something of which Jesus exhorted his disciples and followers often throughout His earthly ministry.

Only true, genuine believers can bear fruit because of their connection to the source of life, Jesus Christ. John 15:1-8 is the quintessential passage on fruit-bearing and ultimately on Christian living.

21. Read **John 15:1-8** and answer the following questions

Who is the vine? _____

Who are the branches? _____

Who is the vinedresser? _____

22. Explain how fruit is produced in the life of the believer.

_____
_____
_____
_____

The disciples would find out later on that they had an example of a fruitless life living and ministering among them, Judas. The life of Judas is somewhat of a paradox. His story leaves you bewildered.

The Bible describes Judas as "the son of perdition" (John 17:12), yet he was chosen by Jesus Christ to be one of the twelve apostles (John 6:70). Judas was given power and authority to perform miracles, to cast out demons, to heal the sick, and to baptize. He was the most trusted among the disciples, with the responsibility of overseeing all financial matters pertaining to the group (John 12:6; 13:29). So trusted was Judas among his fellow disciples that even after Jesus identified him as the one who would later betray Him, they remained totally oblivious.

In the chart below, notice how the actions of Judas identified in John 13 parallel the branch that does not bear fruit illustrated in John 15.

JOHN 13:25-27	JOHN 15:2
"He leaning back thus on Jesus' bosom, said to Him, 'Lord, who is it?' Jesus then answered, 'That is the one for whom I shall dip the morsel and give it to him.' So when He had dipped the morsel, He took and gave it to Judas, the son of Simon Iscariot. After the morsel, Satan entered into him, therefore Jesus said to him, 'What you do, do quickly.'"	"Every branch in Me that does not bear fruit, He takes away....."
JOHN 13:30	JOHN 15:6
"So after receiving the morsel he went out immediately; and it was night."	"If anyone does not abide in me, he is thrown away as a branch and dries up and they gather them and cast them into the fire and they are burned."

Jesus dismissed Judas to his evil deed (John 13:27), just as the vinedresser "takes away" the branch that does not bear fruit.

Judas bore no fruit because there was no life in him. He was like the hardened soil in which the seed could not penetrate.

Although Judas was in the very presence of the Lord Jesus Christ for three years, and heard the Word on numerous occasions, he was not a part of Christ, he could not abide in Christ and therefore he did not bear fruit.

When the Word of God is proclaimed, the expectation is that fruit will be produced in the life of the one who hears it.

> **"By this is My Father glorified that you bear much fruit,
> and so prove to be My disciples."
> John 15:8**

23. What are some concrete steps a woman must take in bearing fruit when faced with the distractions of worry, riches, and desire for other things?

    _____
    _____
    _____
    _____

24. What specific fruit has been borne in your life as a direct result of the Word of God taking root in your heart?

    _____
    _____
    _____
    _____

25. In what areas of life do you know you are barren of fruit but are covering up and excusing?

    _____
    _____
    _____
    _____

O GOD,

May Thy Spirit speak in me that I may speak to thee.
I have no merit, let the merit of Jesus stand for me.
I am undeserving, but I look to Thy tender mercy.
I am full of infirmities, wants, sin; Thou art full of grace.

I confess my sin, my frequent sin, my wilful sin;
all my powers of body and soul are defiled:
a fountain of pollution is deep within my nature.

There are chambers of foul images within my being;
I have gone from one odious room to another,
walked in a no-man's-land of dangerous imaginations,
pried into the secrets of my fallen nature.

I am utterly ashamed that I am what I am in myself;
I have no green shoot in me nor fruit, but thorns and thistles;
I am a fading leaf that the wind drives away;
I live bare and barren as a winter tree, unprofitable,
fit to be hewn down and burnt. Lord, dost Thou have mercy on me?

Thou hast struck a heavy blow at my pride,
at the false god of self, and I lie in pieces before Thee.
But Thou hast given me another master and Lord, Thy Son, Jesus,
and now my heart is turned towards holiness,
my life speeds as an arrow from a bow towards complete obedience to Thee.

Help me in all my doings to put down sin and to humble pride.
Save me from the love of the world and the pride of life,
from everything that is natural to fallen man,
and let Christ's nature be seen in me day by day.
Grant me grace to bear Thy will without repining,
and delight to be not only chiseled, squared, or fashioned,
but separated from the old rock where I have been embedded so long,
and lifted from the quarry to the upper air, where I may be built in Christ for ever.

– The Valley of Vision
Page 73

PERSONAL REFLECTIONS

THE RICH FOOL

THE RICH FOOL

LUKE 12:13-21

"Someone in the crowd said to Him, 'Teacher, tell my brother to divide the family inheritance with me.' But He said to him, 'Man, who appointed Me a judge or arbitrator over you?' Then He said to them, 'Beware, and be on your guard against every form of greed; for not even when one has an abundance does his life consist of his possessions.' And He told them a parable, saying, 'The land of a rich man was very productive.' And he began reasoning to himself, saying, 'What shall I do, since I have no place to store my crops?' Then he said, 'This is what I will do: I will tear down my barns and build larger ones, and there I will store all my grain and my goods. And I will say to my soul, Soul, you have many goods laid up for many years to come; take your ease, eat, drink and be merry.' But God said to him, 'You fool! This very night your soul is required of you; and now who will own what you have prepared?' So is the man who stores up treasure for himself, and is not rich toward God.'"

THE RICH FOOL
Tomorrow Is Not Promised

Theme: The Sinfulness Of Greed

Scripture: Luke 12:13-21

Occasion: Jesus was requested by a listener to settle a family financial matter.

Overview: *Greed*: An on-going and ruthless desire for more of something and a constant obsession with abundance. A greedy person will never say, "What I have is enough!" The parable of the rich fool is an example of the utter sinfulness of greed. Jesus introduces the parable in response to a man who tried to enlist His help in settling a family dispute.

Heart Preparation: "Lord, open my eyes that I may behold wonderful things from Your law and help me to cultivate a heart that consistently treasures Your Word" (Psalm 119:11, 18).

THE RICH FOOL
Tomorrow Is Not Promised

Our Lord Jesus spent most of His earthly ministry teaching about the Kingdom of Heaven and the kingdom-dweller. A part of His teaching focused specifically on the characteristics of the kingdom-dweller's life. The Sermon on the Mount is an example of such. Let's begin our study by reading **Matthew 5:1-16.**

1. List nine characteristics that should be true of every woman of God?

2. Which characteristic stands out to you the most?

3. Which characteristic do you find personally challenging in your walk with the Lord and why?

4. How does materialism and pursuing possessions conflict with kingdom life as Christ defines it in verses 3-16?

5. Read **Luke 12:13-21.** Jot down any thoughts that come to mind.

We do not know if the man in the crowd was a kingdom-dweller. We do know that he was distracted because of a dispute with a family member. We also know that the dispute troubling the man was of a very serious nature, involving the death of his parents and his inheritance.

Unless you are an only child, you can identify with disputes that occur between siblings. I have four brothers and one sister, but I spent most of my childhood years with two of my brothers who are closer to me in age. We certainly had our fair share of disputes and disagreements. Numerous disagreements rose to the level of parental involvement, resulting in long talks about our behavior. An inevitable part of "the talk" would include a stern warning about the underlying issue (sin) that needed to be addressed. My brothers and I listened (or at least looked like we were listening), and afterwards carried on in relative peace and harmony...until the next dispute occurred!

Sometimes family disputes can be long, drawn out, angry, ugly, complicated, and how-can-you-call-yourself-my-brother kind of problems that sadly end up in a courtroom. While you may not have a biological brother (or sister) to fight with, your disputes may be within the family of God, the woman sitting in the pew across from you or the man three rows up from you.

Brothers and sisters in Christ choosing to stand before a judge to settle disputes was one of the numerous problems within the Corinthian church that Paul had to address. Notice what Paul said on the subject.

> **"Do you not know that we will judge angels?**
> **How much more matters of this life?**
> **So if you have law courts dealing with matters of this life,**
> **Do you appoint them as judges who are of no account in the church?**
> **I say this to your shame.**
> **Is it so that there is not among you**
> **One wise man who will be able to decide between his brethren,**
> **But brother goes to law with brother, and that before unbelievers?**
> **Actually then, it is already a defeat for you, that you have lawsuits with one another.**
> **Why not rather be wronged? Why not rather be defrauded?"**
> **I Corinthians 6:3-7**

Perhaps the man in the crowd saw an opportunity in Jesus to get what he wanted. Jesus was a Rabbi and Rabbis were considered by citizens to be qualified to render a settlement on matters such as monetary disputes. He blurted out in the gathering of people being instructed by Jesus and said "tell my brother to divide the family inheritance with me" (Luke 12:13).

The interruption was not to inquire about a theological truth or to ask for help in understanding spiritual things but rather to get something from Jesus. Jesus responded by saying,

> **"Who made me judge and arbitrator over you?"**
> **Luke 12:14**

And immediately to the crowd observing the whole scene Jesus said,

> **"Beware and be on your guard against every form of greed;**
> **For not even when one has an abundance does his life consist of his possessions."**
> **Luke 12:15**

It was a stern and urgent warning not just to the man and the crowd of listeners but to you and me as well. Jesus exposed the man's motive and said "beware and be on your guard." It is the idea of being vigilant over something, in this case "every form of greed." Jesus then illustrated His warning with the Parable of the Rich Fool.

You were asked earlier to jot down some things that came to mind after reading the parable. Perhaps "greed" ranked high on your list. It leaves you speechless that the only thing the rich fool thought to do with his bountiful abundance was to hoard and keep it all to himself. Paul said, "the love of money is a root of all sorts of evil" (I Timothy 6:10).

Greed is evil and it makes you do evil things. A greedy person is almost always a covetous person. Greed and covetousness are very closely tied. If life was a game, covetousness would get you to "suit up" and greed would keep you in play.

In Proverbs 27:17 we are told that iron sharpens iron. However in this case, covetousness sharpens greed. The more you covet, the greedier you become. Attitudes of discontentment, ungratefulness, selfishness, pride, and a sense of entitlement fuel the flames of sinful desires from which greed becomes more prominent.

The Parable of the Rich Fool demonstrates each of these sinful attitudes and it offers a very sad example of what can happen when greed dominates a person's heart.

6. Before going further in the parable, read the following verses and take note of what God says about greed and covetousness. Write your thoughts on the lines provided.

   A.   **Ephesians 5:3-5**

   _____
   _____
   _____

   B.   **Colossians 3:5**

   _____
   _____
   _____

   C.   **Romans 13:9**

   _____
   _____
   _____

   D.   **Psalm 10:3**

   _____
   _____
   _____

   E.   **Mark 7:20-23**

   _____
   _____
   _____

   F.   **I Corinthians 5:11**

   _____
   _____
   _____

The rich man Jesus described in the parable, owned land that produced an overwhelming supply of crops. The land was very productive (Luke 12:16). The land produced more than the man had ever experienced in his farming career. He immediately began contemplating what to do with it all.

Luke 12:17-19 indicates why Jesus also described the rich man as a fool. Keep in mind that, although Jesus characterized him as a fool, it does not mean that he was unintelligent or uneducated. Most likely he was a well educated and intelligent man. He was apparently very skilled in farming and the agricultural industry, evidenced in the fact that he was wealthy prior to the massive production of crops.

The Greek word for fool used in this parable is *aphron*,[1] meaning "senseless; deficient perception of value and truth." The rich fool put value in that which was valueless and put no value in that which was most valuable.

The problem was not that the man was wealthy. Jesus was not condemning wealth or the possession of wealth. Jesus was not condemning financial gain and increase through legitimate and successful means. In fact, the first verse of the parable is exciting news.

> **"The land of a rich man was very productive."**
> **Luke 12:16**

That is wonderful. That is great. That is celebratory. Jesus had no problem with the man experiencing an abundance of crop. The problem arises when the man began reasoning to himself. The rich fool's decision concerning his wealth was what Jesus condemned.

Read again **Luke 12:17-19** and take note of the number of personal pronouns used.

> **"And he began reasoning to himself, saying,**
> **'What shall I do, since I have no place to store my crops?'**
> **Then he said, 'This is what I will do:**
> **I will tear down my barns and build larger ones,**
> **And there I will store all my grain and my goods.**
> **And I will say to my soul,**
> **Soul, you have many goods laid up for many years to come;**
> **Take your ease, eat, drink and be merry.'"**
> **Luke 12:17-19**

Depending on the version of Scripture you are using, there are at least thirteen personal pronouns. Think about that for a moment. No less than thirteen times the rich man proudly spoke of the increase as if it came from his own ingenuity.

---

[1] Verlyn Verbrugge. *The NIV Theological Dictionary Of New Testament Words*, Grand Rapids, MI. Zondervan Publishing House, 2000, 848.

Mysteries of the Kingdom Revealed

No less than thirteen times the rich man laid claim to what ultimately belonged to God. No less than thirteen times the rich man failed to honor and give glory and thanksgiving to God. Instead he sinned against God, the very One who had blessed him so abundantly.

Oh, how the story would have been different if the rich man, upon receiving the excess crop, had stopped whatever he was doing, knelt down and prayed as David once prayed. Read **I Chronicles 29:11-12** and write David's prayer below.

_____
_____
_____
_____
_____
_____
_____

But unfortunately, the unthinkable happened. The statement by the rich fool of what he planned to do with his riches was stunning and yet another reminder of the sinfulness of sin. There is nothing more selfish and sinful than to have an abundance and respond by tightening your grip all the more.

Solomon warns against that kind of mind set in Proverbs.

> **"There is one who scatters, and yet increases all the more,
> And there is one who withholds what is justly due,
> and yet it results only in want.
> The generous man will be prosperous,
> And he who waters will himself be watered.
> He who withholds grain, the people will curse him,
> But blessing will be on the head of him who sells it.
> He who diligently seeks good seeks favor,
> But he who seeks evil, evil will come to him.
> He who trusts in his riches will fall,
> But the righteous will flourish like the green leaf."
> Proverbs 11:24-28**

Perhaps the Psalmist had individuals like the rich fool in mind when he said,

> **"A fool says in his heart, 'there is no God."
> Psalm 14:1**

It is not that the fool in Psalm 14 does not believe in the existence of God, but rather the individual lives life with "no need for God" as his mantra.

Often when we hear of someone talking like a fool or acting foolishly, we think in terms of stupidity or recklessness. However, the behavior of the rich man in the parable was not about an intellectual deficiency but rather a moral deficiency. Jesus did not characterize the man as a fool because he was willfully ignorant but because the man was morally wrong in how he viewed life (and death, for that matter). He had no regard for God; he had no regard for others; and he had no regard for his own mortality. He was alone. He talked to himself. He consulted with himself. He decided to forecast his future only to find out that God had other plans.

The lust of the flesh, the lust of the eyes, and the boastful pride of life (I John 2:15-16) are all manifested in this man. God hates pride. It is an abomination to Him (Proverbs 6:17). Boasting out of a heart filled with pride leaves God out. It makes you believe that you are somehow in control of your life. It blinds you to the fact that life is fragile and the very next breath could be your last.

Listen to the warning given by James.

> **"Come now, you who say,**
> **'Today or tomorrow we will go to such and such a city,**
> **And spend a year there and engage in business and make a profit.'**
> **Yet you do not know what your life will be like tomorrow.**
> **You are just a vapor that appears for a little while and then vanishes away.**
> **Instead you ought to say,**
> **'If the Lord wills, we will live and also do this or that.'**
> **But as it is, you boast in your arrogance, all such boasting is evil."**
> **James 4:13-16**

7. What does Paul say about boasting in **I Corinthians 4:7**? Write your thoughts below.

_____
_____
_____
_____

There was another fool in the Old Testament who also responded sinfully to the goodness of the Lord. But that fool was married to a beautiful woman who helped spare his life after he made a foolish and deadly decision.

Read the story of Abigail and Nabal in **I Samuel 25:1-38.**

8. Write down 3 things that Abigail did that helped to spare her husband's life.

_____
_____
_____
_____
_____
_____
_____

9. What similarities do you see between Nabal and the rich fool in Luke 12:13-21. Write your thoughts below.

_____
_____
_____
_____
_____
_____
_____

The rich fool, in contemplating all he would do with his excess wealth, summed it up in five words, "Eat, drink and be merry." But he would never see or experience one minute of his acclaimed life of ease because of what happened in the very next verse.
God spoke to him. Don't miss that! The Bible says in Luke 12:20, "but God said to him."

These are the most powerful and important words in the entire parable. The fact that Jesus would include God the Father speaking in a parable is profound. It would have been shocking to the people listening, given the fact that the man was godless. What this communicates is that although the rich fool did not acknowledge God, God was very much aware of him, of what he said, of what he did and was planning to do.

As he finalized the plans regarding his bountiful riches, he heard God say,

**"You fool! This very night your soul is required of you;
And now who will own what you have prepared?"
Luke 12:20**

The Rich Fool

10. Read **Ezekiel 18:4** and write it on the lines below.

_____
_____
_____
_____
_____

11. Read **Matthew 16:26** and write it on the lines below.

_____
_____
_____
_____
_____

Your soul belongs to God. Even if you could gain the whole world, even if you could own everything, it wouldn't change the fact that your soul belongs to God... always has and always will. He has the right to take it back whenever He chooses. For the rich fool, it happened the very same night his land produced an enormous crop. Unbeknownst to the man, he was making plans and preparations for a day and time that he would never see.

In conclusion, as a believer reading the Parable of the Rich Fool, I notice the fact that God can extend mercy and grace even in times of judgment. God said to the rich fool, "...this very night your soul is required of you." God could have said "this very moment your soul is required of you" and the man could have breathed his last breath.

It reminds me of a true story that occurred in the book of Acts. The story is about the actions of a couple whose greed and covetousness, along with lies and deception, brought on the swift judgment of God. Although God did not speak audibly to the couple, He did speak through the Apostle Peter. You know this to be Ananias and Sapphira who "agreed together to put the Spirit of the Lord to the test" (Acts 5:9). Read their story in Acts 5:1-11 and take notice of what happened to Sapphira after she chose to continue the deceptive plot.

Unlike Ananias, God extended grace to Sapphira in that He gave her two opportunities to abandon the evil deed and to be truthful. Acts 5:7 states that a period of three hours had elapsed before Sapphira was questioned by Peter. God gave her three hours to consider, or rather reconsider, what she and her husband had concocted. Also notice that Peter asked specifically about the price of the land, once again giving Sapphira an opportunity to be forthright; but to her demise she lied. No sooner did the lie roll off her tongue that she breathed her last breath and died. Just like Sapphira, the rich fool in the parable was given opportunity.

Nightfall had not yet occurred which meant there was still time for him to turn in repentance from his evil and selfish ways and to acknowledge God for who He is. There was yet still time for the man to confess his sin before a righteous and holy God and ask for forgiveness.

12. How can we as women guard ourselves against "every form of greed?"

13. Does the social media arena play a roll in feeding our greed? If so, in what ways?

14. What are some common characteristics of greed displayed in a woman's life?

15. How does the culture create an environment for women to desire and pursue more rather than being satisfied with what they have?

16. What are some ways that one can be "rich toward God" that do not necessarily involve money?

17. How are you managing what has been entrusted to you so as to be rich toward God?

_____
_____
_____
_____

18. What challenges do you face personally in being rich toward God with your time, talents, and resources?

_____
_____
_____
_____

What we know for sure about the rich fool:

- He was a farmer.
- He was wealthy prior to experiencing a "very productive" crop.
- He did nothing out of the ordinary to achieve the excess that occurred.
- He had no control over the results of the crop once planted.
- His wealth and additional prosperity came directly from the providential hand of God.
- He failed to acknowledge that God alone controls the elements and all the factors that go into farming.
- He failed to acknowledge that God alone has the power to produce wealth.
- He was judged for his sinful presumption.

Jesus concluded the Parable of the Rich Fool with one final warning to the people who were listening to Him and to you and me as well. Jesus said,

"So is the man who stores up treasure for himself and is not rich toward God."
Luke 12:21

The one who chooses to set their affections and efforts in life on acquiring wealth rather than being rich toward God is a fool. Just as greed and covetousness are closely tied, your heart and your treasure are also closely tied. Jesus mentioned this fact at the end of the chapter when He said,

"Where your treasure is there your heart will be also."
Luke 12:34

O LORD,

I am a shell full of dust,
but animated with an invisible rational soul
and made anew by an unseen power of grace;

I am deeply convinced
of the evil and misery of my sinful state,
of the vanity of creatures,
but also of the sufficiency of Christ.

When You would guide me I control myself,
When You would be sovereign I rule myself,
When You would take care of me I suffice myself.
When I should depend on Your providings I supply myself,
When I should submit to Your providence I follow my will,
When I should study, love, honour, trust thee, I serve myself;
I fault and correct thy laws to suit myself,
Instead of thee I look to a man's approval,
and am by nature an idolater.

Lord, it is my chief design to bring my heart back to thee.
Convince me that I cannot be my own God, or make myself happy,
nor my own Christ to restore my joy,
nor my own Spirit to teach, guide, rule me.

Help me to see that grace does this by providential affliction.

Take away my roving eye, curious ear, greedy appetite, lustful heart;
show me that none of these things
can heal a wounded conscience,
or support a tottering frame,
or uphold a departing spirit.

Then take me to the cross and leave me there.

– The Valley of Vision
Page 91

PERSONAL REFLECTIONS

THE UNMERCIFUL SERVANT

THE UNMERCIFUL SERVANT

(MATTHEW 18:21-35)

"Then Peter came and said to Him, 'Lord, how often shall my brother sin against me and I forgive him? Up to seven times?' Jesus said to him, 'I do not say to you up to seven times, but up to seventy times seven.' For this reason the kingdom of heaven may be compared to a king who wished to settle accounts with his slaves. When he had begun to settle them, one who owed him ten thousand talents was brought to him. But since he did not have the means to repay, his lord commanded him to be sold, along with his wife and children and all that he had, and repayment to be made. So the slave fell to the ground and prostrated himself before him, saying, 'Have patience with me and I will repay you everything.' And the lord of that slave felt compassion and released him and forgave him the debt. But that slave went out and found one of his fellow slaves who owed him a hundred denarii; and he seized him and began to choke him, saying, 'Pay back what you owe.' So his fellow slave fell to the ground and began to plead with him, saying, 'Have patience with me and I will repay you.' But he was unwilling and went and threw him in prison until he should pay back what was owed. So when his fellow slaves saw what had happened, they were deeply grieved and came and reported to their lord all that had happened. Then summoning him, his lord said to him, 'You wicked slave, I forgave you all that debt because you pleaded with me. Should you not also have had mercy on your fellow slave, in the same way that I had mercy on you?' And his lord, moved with anger, handed him over to the torturers until he should repay all that was owed him. My heavenly Father will also do the same to you, if each of you does not forgive his brother from your heart."

THE UNMERCIFUL SERVANT
Unforgiveness

Theme: Forgiveness From The Heart

Scripture: Matthew 18:21-35

Occasion: Peter asked Jesus a question about forgiveness.

Overview: "A man's discretion makes him slow to anger, and it is his glory to overlook a transgression" (Proverbs 19:11). Jesus tells a parable about a man with an incalculable debt who pleaded for the king's patience. Instead of patience, the king responded with compassion and forgave the man of the entire debt. However, the man's unreasonable and unmerciful behavior toward a fellow servant was what caused him to be handed over to the "torturers."

Heart Preparation: "How blessed is he whose transgression is forgiven, whose sin is covered! How blessed is the man to whom the Lord does not impute iniquity, and in whose spirit there is no deceit" (Psalm 32:1-2)!

THE UNMERCIFUL SERVANT
Unforgiveness

Never are you more like God than when you forgive
– Dr. John MacArthur

"The Brave One"   "Man On Fire"
"The Count of Monte Cristo"   "The Punisher"
"Payback"   "True Grit"
"Kill Bill   "V for Vendetta"
"Law Abiding Citizen"   "Lady Vengeance"

You might be wondering why I have begun the lesson with a list of movie titles. If you are familiar with or have actually watched any of the aforementioned movies, you know that forgiveness was not what the movie promoted. Some movie titles such as "Lady Vengeance" and "Payback" leave no doubt in your mind that the theme of the movie is pure revenge.

Revenge seeks to desecrate and devour. It will drive you to hurt an innocent person if it causes pain and suffering to your intended victim. Your desire is to inflict far worse pain than what was inflicted on you, which is the nature of revenge.

For example, in the movie "The Punisher," a couple's son is accidentally killed during a drug bust. The couple avenges their son's death by murdering the entire family (women, children, infants and grandparents) of a federal agent who set up the drug bust. Neither the federal agent nor his family members had anything to do with the accidental death of the couple's son. Revenge seeks to cause greater suffering on the target. However, revenge often seems just.

As believers God has given us a direct command against acts of revenge and retaliation. Paul said, "<u>Never</u> take your own revenge beloved, but leave room for the wrath of God, for it is written, 'Vengence is Mine, I will repay,' says the Lord" (Romans 12:19). Instead of revenge, God commands us to forbear and forgive (Colossians 3:13).

But how? How can a person forgive someone who has hurt them? How can a person forgive someone who has violated or injured them or their loved one? What about repeat offenders such as, the woman on your job, at your child's school, in your church or perhaps in your family, who has offended you on more than one occasion. Does God expect total forgiveness in any situation? Is there an occasion when forgiveness cannot be granted? Is it ever okay to withhold forgiveness?

Mysteries of the Kingdom Revealed

In Matthew 18, the disciples were getting ready to be taught a difficult lesson on forgiveness. After teaching on what it means to have child-like faith, Jesus gave instruction on church discipline. He taught them how to respond when a brother sins against them. Peter listened and immediately asked a question that perhaps many of the other disciples had on their mind as well. It was a question that you and I most likely would have wanted to know. The question centered on how often forgiveness was to be granted to the one who sins against you.

1. Before we continue with the parable, on the lines below, define forgiveness. What is forgiveness and how is it to be accomplished?

_____
_____
_____
_____
_____
_____
_____

> **"Then Peter came and said to Him,**
> **'Lord, how often shall my brother sin against me and I forgive him?**
> **Up to seven times?' Jesus said to him,**
> **'I do not say to you, up to seven times, but up to seventy times seven.'"**
> **Matthew 18:21-22**

Peter asked Jesus if forgiving someone seven times was sufficient. Jesus' answer was most likely shocking to Peter and the disciples. That an individual could keep a record of multiple offenses up to a whopping 490 times was an impossible scenario. Jesus' point was that only one kind of forgiveness was acceptable to God, forgiveness offered freely from the heart.

Jesus followed up His answer with a parable illustrating how forgiveness from the heart is accomplished as well as the horrible consequences of unforgiveness. Peter and the other disciples needed to understand that forgiveness was not about calculating a number but rather extending to others what had been lavishly extended to them.

> **"For this reason the kingdom of heaven may be compared to a king**
> **Who wished to settle accounts with his slaves. When he had begun to settle them,**
> **One who owed him ten thousand talents was brought to him.**

**But since he did not have the means to repay,
His lord commanded him to be sold
Along with his wife and children and all that he had and repayment to be made.
So the slave fell to the ground and prostrated himself before him saying,
'Have patience with me and I will repay you everything.'
And the lord of that slave felt compassion
And released him and forgave him the debt."
Matthew 18:23-27**

2. What are your observations? Who are the main characters and what is their relationship to each other? Who are the characters representing?

_____
_____
_____
_____
_____
_____

Many of Jesus' parables were illustrations of what the kingdom of heaven would be like. The disciples would have been familiar with the idea of a king returning from a long journey and settling accounts he had left in his servant's charge.

> "A 'talent' is a measurement of weight of gold, silver, or copper.
> It varied but was between approximately 60 and 90 pounds.
> Ten thousand talents would be about 204 metric tons. Depending
> on which metal was used, a talent was the equivalent of about
> 6000 denarii, which would make the first servants debt 60,000,000
> denarii, and at one denarius a day (as in Matt. 20:2) would require
> a day laborer over 164,000 years to repay."[1]

Jesus purposely chose an outrageously high number. How the servant accumulated the enormity of debt is unknown. However, the master proceeded to exercise his legal right to have the servant, his wife, and his children sold into slavery as well as the servant's possessions seized. This was typically the next step when attempting to recover debt.

The servant wasted no time in falling to the floor, prostrated before his master. He pleaded with his master to be patient and assured him that he would repay all that was owed.

---

[1] Klyne R. Snodgrass. *Stories With Intent*; Wm. B. Eerdmans Publishing Co., Grand Rapids/Cambridge 66.

Mysteries of the Kingdom Revealed

Though the servant vowed to pay back all he owed, it was never going to happen. It was impossible. The exorbitant amount of debt could not be repaid. Selling himself, his wife and their children into slavery would do nothing towards alleviating the debt. Clearly this was a hopeless and desperate situation in which the servant found himself.

Think about how the events in the story thus far parallel perfectly with the lot of mankind prior to salvation. Words like hopeless, desperate, impossible to escape, all describe our state prior to Christ. We also had an incalculable debt that we could not pay. But God!

3. Look up the following verses and jot down the impact "But God" makes in the lives of believers.

    A. **Ephesians 2:1-6**

    B. **Romans 5:8-10**

    C. **Colossians 2:13-14**

    D. **II Corinthians 7:5-6**

    E. **Psalm 73:26**

Out of the kindness of his heart the merciful master forgave his servant. He was asked by the servant to be patient however, patience would not have solved the problem. What was needed was granted: compassion, mercy, and forgiveness!

One can not imagine the emotional high and exhilaration that the servant must have felt upon hearing that his debt had been expunged.

You would expect the servant to have been in utter shock and disbelief, perhaps wondering if he had heard correctly. You would expect the servant to have been thinking about his wife and children no longer on the brink of enslavement because in an instant their situation was changed. You would expect the servant to have been thinking about his future and the wonderful opportunities he might experience with financial freedom. You would expect the servant to be fighting back tears over the sheer enormity of the debt he had amassed but also of joy and gratitude because of the great mercy he had been shown.

What you would **not** expect of the servant are the actions that transpired in the following verses.

> **28 "But that slave went out and found one of his fellow slaves who owed him a hundred denarii.
> And he seized him and began to choke him saying, 'Pay back what you owe me!'
> 29 His fellow slave fell to the ground and began to plead with him, saying 'Have patience with me, and I will repay you.'"
> Matthew 18:28-29**

4. What are your observations regarding these verses? What are the similarities and differences between these verses and verses 26-27? Who are the characters? Who are the characters representing?

_____
_____
_____
_____
_____
_____
_____

This is outrageous! The servant who had just been forgiven an unimaginable amount of debt left the presence of his master and immediately found a fellow slave. "He seized him and began to choke him" describes a very angry and violent encounter.

What adds to the egregious nature of his actions was the fact that the fellow slave owed a reasonable amount of debt and repayment was certainly plausible. The forgiven slave, perhaps out of desperation, lied and suggested that he could pay back what was owed if given time. However in reality, his debt could not and would not have been repaid in several lifetimes. In comparison, the amount of debt owed by the second slave (one hundred denarii) was the equivalent of a few thousand dollars. It was a manageable debt.

> "A denarii was a day's wage for a common laborer, so that was approximately a third of a year's wages. Assuming (in our terms) that a low wage might be twelve or fifteen thousand dollars per year, it was only four or five thousand dollars. That was a significant amount of money, but it was a pittance compared to the enormous debt the first servant had incurred."[2]

Everything about the forgiven slave's behavior toward his fellow slave was ruthless and unwarranted. It was completely inconsistent with what you would expect of someone who had been shown such kindness and mercy.

Notice that the fellow slave pleaded in the exact same manner, using the exact same wording as the forgiven slave (Matthew 18:29). Yet it did nothing to soften the forgiven slave's harsh actions. It seemed as if he was determined to inflict extreme suffering and harm to his fellow slave. Why? Why did he not show mercy to his fellow slave? Why did he refuse to forgive his fellow slave of the debt just as he had been forgiven?

**30 "But he was unwilling and went and threw him in prison
until he should pay back what was owed."
Matthew 18:30**

You wonder if the emotions of the disciples were running pretty high as they listened to the story intensify.

How could an individual, after experiencing overwhelming compassion and love be so full of anger and contempt toward a fellow slave? An unforgiving spirit is completely devoid of mercy and desires swift judgment on the offender. Without mercy, forgiveness is impossible.

---

[2] James Montgomery Boice. *The Parables of Jesus*, Moody Publishers, 1983, 212.

Let's take a moment and consider mercy. What is mercy? There are several words from both Hebrew and Greek texts that are associated with God's mercy as shown below.

Kapporeth	"ransom," "propitiatory," or "the mercy seat"
Racham	"to love," "to have compassion," or "to show mercy"
Chesed	"goodness," "kindness," "mercifulness," or "loving-kindness"
Eleemon	"to show mercy," "to pity," "to have compassion" or "to be merciful"
Oiktirmos	"compassion" or "pity"[3]

Take note of the definitions of mercy by the following theologians:

Millard Erickson	Martin Luther	Jonathan Edwards	Charles Hodge
"God's mercy is his tenderhearted, loving compassion for his people. It is his tenderness of heart toward the needy. If grace contemplates humans as sinful, guilty, and condemned, mercy sees them as miserable and needy."	"This is the first work of God—that He is merciful to all who are ready to do without their own opinion, right, wisdom, and all spiritual goods, and willing to be poor in spirit."	"God is pleased to show mercy to his enemies, according to his own sovereign pleasure. Though He is infinitely above all, and stands in no need of creatures; yet he is graciously pleased to take a merciful notice of poor worms in the dust."	"Mercy is kindness exercised toward the miserable, and includes pity, compassion, forbearance, and gentleness, which the Scriptures so abundantly ascribe to God."[4]

5. With the above information in mind, how do you define mercy? Write your thoughts below including any scriptures that support your definition.

_____
_____
_____
_____

---

[3] http://www.allaboutgod.com/what-is-mercy-faq.htm

[4] Ibid

Mysteries of the Kingdom Revealed

6. In the chart below are the stories of three nameless women to whom Jesus extended mercy. Read their stories and make a list of what you learn about mercy.

Adulterous Woman (John 8:1-11)	Sinful Woman (Luke 7:36-50)	Woman At The Well (John 4:1-29)

**"So when his fellow slaves saw what had happened,
they were deeply grieved and
came and reported to their lord all that had happened.
Then summoning him, his lord said to him,
'You wicked slave, I forgave you all that debt because you pleaded with me.
Should you not also have had mercy on your fellow slave,
In the same way that I had mercy on you?'
And his lord moved with anger handed him over to the torturers
until he should repay all that was owed him."
Matthew 18:31-34**

7. What are your observations? Who are the main characters and what is their relationship to each other? Who are the characters representing?

_____
_____
_____
_____
_____

We would agree that the forgiven slave should have been eager to forgive. We would agree that the forgiven slave should have passed along the mercy and kindness he had graciously received. We would agree that the forgiven slave was justly punished for the brutal way he treated his fellow slave. However, you may be thinking that Jesus used an extreme example to make His point about forgiveness. You may also be thinking that your situation is different and the hurt you are experiencing due to being sinned against is sometimes paralyzing. You may even be thinking that your unwillingness to forgive your offender is justified.

**"My heavenly Father will also do the same to you,
if each of you does not forgive his brother from your heart."
Matthew 18:35**

8. What do you think Jesus meant when he said, "My heavenly Father will also do **the same to you** if each of you does not forgive his brother **from your heart**.

_____
_____
_____

*To dwell above with the Saints we love
will be grace and glory
but to live below with the Saints we know,
that's a different story.*
– Anonymous

Euodia and Syntyche, who had once ministered alongside the Apostle Paul, were urged by him to "live in harmony in the Lord" (Philippians 4:1-3). What happened in their relationship that disrupted the harmony they once experienced? Whose fault was it? Were they able to resolve their differences and how were they resolved? Was the relationship restored? How did the church respond? Did the two ladies continue to minister in the church of Philippi? So many questions.

Apparently God did not feel it was necessary for us to know specific details about what happened between Euodia and Syntyche.

Broken relationships are often the result of unforgiveness. There is nothing more detrimental to the unity among believers than unforgiveness. Pride, anger, bitterness and resentment are some of the emotions that fill our heart when we feel we have been wronged. The more the offense is rehearsed and mulled over in our mind, the stronger the feelings become. Forgiveness from the heart is virtually impossible until the sinful emotions are dealt with biblically.

Just the opposite is true of restored relationships. Rather than pride, humility fills the heart. Rather than anger, bitterness, and resentment; holiness, genuine love and compassion fill the heart. All of these are anchored in mercy. Forgiveness from the heart is to allow mercy to triumph.

The Bible gives us a powerful example of how forgiveness from the heart can lead to restored relationships.

The story of Joseph demonstrates that anger, bitterness, and resentment do not have to control our response when sinned against or treated wrongly. You do not have to be overcome by evil, you can overcome evil with good (Romans 12:21).

Joseph's story spans thirteen chapters. It begins in Genesis 37 and picks up again in chapters 39-50. Like the varicolored coat given to him by his father, Joseph's life experiences were varied. It was at the age of seventeen and in full view of his eleven brothers that Joseph was shown to be the favored son.

Presented with a uniquely designed tunic, also called an ornamented coat: (coat of many colors),[5] Joseph's presence was a constant reminder to his brothers of the special position he held in their father's heart. Joseph was their father's favorite. He was the eldest son of the woman Jacob loved, Rachel. It was obvious to the brothers that they were second in their father's heart. The brothers, to be expected, hated Joseph and wanted him dead.

Take note of what Joseph endured because of his brothers hatred of him:
- Attacked by his brothers (37:23)
- Thrown in a pit (37:24)
- Sold to traders (37:28)
- Taken to Egypt (37:28)
- Bought by Potiphar (37:36, 39:1)

---

[5]Charles Caldwell Ryrie, Ph.D., *Ryrie Study Bible*. Moody Press, Chicago

- Forced to be a slave in Potiphar's house (39:2-4)
- Seduced by Potiphar's wife (39:7, 10)
- Falsely accused by Potiphar's wife (39:17-18)
- Convicted solely on the false claims of Potiphar's wife (39:20)
- Imprisoned (39:20)

9. In spite of all Joseph endured at the hands of his brothers, he maintained a godly perspective. Read **Genesis 50:19-20** and write it on the lines below.

_____
_____
_____
_____
_____
_____

The way in which Joseph responded to the severe adversity in his life evidenced the humility, holiness, genuine love and compassion in his heart. Without these, the story of Joseph would have been very different from what was recorded in scripture.

10. Read **Genesis 50:21**. How did Joseph demonstrate forgiveness?

_____
_____
_____
_____
_____

Why do we desperately struggle with forgiving when wronged? Why is forgiving from the heart so difficult? Why do we sometimes refuse to forgive? Why is forgiveness a subject we would rather not discuss?

We struggle with forgiveness because we attempt to do in the flesh what can only be done by the Spirit. Forgiveness is a spiritual act in which a pardoning of the offender's sin is willingly granted by the offended. Therefore, if forgiveness is attempted in the flesh it will fail. Our sinful flesh does not want to forgive. Our sinful flesh does not want to do anything that God has commanded.

> **"For the mind set on the flesh is hostile toward God**
> **and it does not subject itself to the law of God,**
> **for it is not even able to do so."**
> **Romans 8:7**

11. According to Galatians 2:20, what must happen in a person's life in order to change their disposition from hostility towards God to obedience to God?

_____
_____
_____
_____

Notice what Paul wrote in his letter to the Galatians:

> **"The flesh sets its desire against the Spirit, and the Spirit against the flesh; for these are in opposition to one another, so that you may not do the things that you please."**
> **Galatians 5:17**

Sometimes our struggle with forgiving from the heart is because we are operating under misconceptions about forgiveness. Let's look at a few.

MISCONCEPTIONS OF FORGIVENESS

Forgiveness can not be granted if you do not feel like forgiving.

Forgiveness is not a feeling, it is a choice. To forgive only when you feel like forgiving is to be an unforgiving person. As parents we forgive our children all the time. We may not always feel like forgiving them, but we do it because they are our children and we love them. I can say with a high level of confidence that throughout the course of a day you have acted in spite of your feelings. The same is true of me. As Christians we are commanded to "walk by faith" not according to feelings (II Corinthians 5:7).

It is faulty to believe you cannot forgive until you feel like forgiving. Through Christ, you can forgive even though your feelings may not agree.

Forgiveness is a choice in which, in willing obedience to the Lord God, you forgive the one who has sinned against you. Forgiveness is to choose to act towards your offender in mercy and kindness rather than revenge and ill treatment.

1. What do the following verses teach about relying on feelings as a guide? Relate what you learn to the following statement: "I will forgive when I feel I am ready to forgive."

A. **Proverbs 28:26**

B. **Proverbs 14:12-13**

C. **Proverbs 3:5-6**

D. **Proverbs 16:2**

E. **Jeremiah 10:23**

Forgiveness means to forget what happened that caused the hurt.

God told the children of Israel through the prophet Isaiah, "I will not remember your sins" (Is. 43:25). Does this mean that God is forgetful? Does this mean that God expects you and me to forget the sins others commit against us?

Forgiveness does not mean you will automatically forget the offense perpetrated against you. While in time you may forget, you are not sinning against God because you have memories about what caused the hurt and pain in your life. You and I sin against God when we choose not to forgive, or when we forgive and later bring up the offense to that person.

God is omniscient which means He has total and complete knowledge of everything, all the time and for all time! He knows all things perfectly and His knowledge is limitless. He can never be unaware of something or come to learn something. "Who has directed

Mysteries of the Kingdom Revealed

the Spirit of the Lord, or as His counselor has informed Him" (Is. 40:13)? The answer: no one! How can an all-powerful, all-knowing God forget the sins you and I have committed, sins that required the death, burial, and resurrection of His beloved Son?

When God said He will not remember our sins, it means that because of Christ's perfect sacrifice, which paid our sin debt, God declared us righteous and **chooses not to hold our sins against us**. Therefore, He will not punish us as we deserve but has removed our sin "as far as the east is from the west" (Psalm 103:12).

2. As a believer, how does it make you feel that God chooses not to hold your sins against you?

   _____
   _____
   _____
   _____

Forgiveness and reconciliation are the same.

Forgiveness and reconciliation are not the same. "I forgive you" does not mean "I trust you." Trust must be earned over time. "I forgive you" does not mean we are back to being buddies, nor does it mean the relationship picks up where it left off. God has not commanded us to become best buddies. He has commanded, "If possible, so far as it depends on you, be at peace with all men" (Romans 12:18). Some relationships may not be the same after an offense has occurred. Yet other relationships are rebuilt over a period of time and become stronger.

Read **Matthew 5:23-24.**

3. What is the believer's responsibility when a relationship has been fractured?

   _____
   _____
   _____

Read **Acts 15:36-40**.

4. What was the problem that caused the separation of Paul and Barnabas?

   _____
   _____
   _____

5. What are your thoughts about how Paul and Barnabas handled the situation? How could it have been handled differently?

_____
_____
_____

Read **II Timothy 4:9-11**. Several years later, Paul asked that John Mark be brought to him to help in ministry.

6. What does Paul's change of heart concerning John Mark teach you about reconciliation and unity?

_____
_____
_____

7. How can we as sisters in Christ be on guard against the tendency to separate over disagreements?

_____
_____
_____

Forgiveness cannot be granted unless the offender asks to be forgiven

There are some who believe the Bible only teaches that forgiveness is conditional and therefore cannot be granted unilaterally. They believe that since God forgives only those who repent, we as believers are not to forgive one another until repentance has been established. The offender confesses and repents, while the offended promises never to bring up the offense, and a "transaction" takes place.

One major flaw with this kind of thinking is that it is devoid of mercy. Rather than an attitude of mercy, an attitude of entitlement (You owe me!) dominates. Another major flaw with this kind of thinking is that it does not take Jesus' example of forgiveness into consideration, for Jesus Himself at times forgave unilaterally. One such occasion involves a woman who was crying on His feet. At first, Jesus did not say a word to her but instead spoke to Simon the Pharisee who had vitriol in his heart towards the woman. Jesus rebuked Simon and by the end of the conversation, although the woman spoke no words, Jesus said to her, "your sins have been forgiven" (Luke 7:36-48). Unilateral forgiveness! Jesus forgave the woman unilaterally. That's the mercy of God. It is the same mercy He expects you and me to extend to one another.

Another example of unilateral forgiveness occurred in Acts 7. Stephen as he was pelted with large stones, "cried out with a loud voice, 'Lord, do not hold this sin against them'" (Acts 7:60). In the midst of dying, Stephen forgave his murderers.
Our Lord Jesus Christ said on the cross, "Father, forgive them, for they know not what they do" (Luke 23:34)!

This is not to say that there will never be situations when confrontation and repentance must occur before forgiveness can be extended. Conditional forgiveness is biblical forgiveness, but it is not the only kind of forgiveness. Conditional forgiveness is understood to be what is inferred from the following verses.

> **"Be kind to one another, tender-hearted, forgiving each other, just as God in Christ also has forgiven you" (Ephesians 4:32).**
>
> **"...bearing with one another, and forgiving each other, whoever has a complaint against anyone; just as the Lord forgave you, so also should you" (Colossians 3:13).**

However, forgiveness can and should be granted unilaterally at times. When the Word of God commands believers to forgive as God has forgiven, withholding forgiveness was not the goal. In fact, to withhold forgiveness would seem to bring judgment according to the following verses. Notice what is said:

> **"For if you forgive others for their transgressions, Your heavenly Father will also forgive you. But if you do not forgive others, Then your Father will not forgive your transgressions."**
> **Matthew 6:14-15**
>
> **"Whenever you stand praying, forgive, If you have anything against anyone, so that your Father Who is in heaven will also forgive you your transgressions. But if you do not forgive, neither will your Father Who is in heaven forgive your transgressions."**
> **Mark 11:25-26**
>
> **"My heavenly Father will also do the same to you, If each of you does not forgive His brother from your heart."**
> **Matthew 18:35**

The parable of the unmerciful servant clearly illustrates unilateral forgiveness. Let's review the parable. Read again **Matthew 18:23-27**.

8. What specifically did the slave ask of the king?

    _____
    _____
    _____

9. What did the slave receive from the king though he did not ask?

    _____

10. What prompted the king to respond to the offense the way in which he did?

    _____
    _____
    _____

There was no indication that the king was under duress when he made the decision to forgive the slave his debt. There was no mention of a transaction in which certain terms had to be met by the slave in order for forgiveness to be granted by the king. In fact, the slave did not ask the king to forgive the debt, but only to give him time to repay it.

What the king did in the parable was done freely, willingly and magnanimously. He forgave the slave entirely. No portion of the debt was to be collected at a later date. The slave immediately was free.

This is one example of forgiveness we are to follow. The gospel of Luke says it like this:

> **"Be merciful, just as your Father is merciful.**
> **Do not judge, and you will not be judged;**
> **And do not condemn, and you will not be condemned;**
> **Pardon, and you will be pardoned.**
> **Give, and it will be given to you.**
> **They will pour into your lap a good measure,**
> **Pressed down, shaken together, and running over.**
> **For by your standard of measure it will be measured to you in return."**
> **Luke 6:36-38**

Another example of forgiveness is also found in the gospel of Luke. Notice what is said,

> **"Be on your guard! If your brother sins, rebuke him;**
> **And if he repents, forgive him.**
> **And if he sins against you seven times a day,**
> **And returns to you seven times, saying,**
> **'I repent,' forgive him."**
> **Luke 17:3-4**

To some, these two passages in Luke 17 are viewed as the only pattern upon which forgiveness is to be offered. If an offender does not confess and repent of their sin, some believe that forgiveness is to be withheld. These two verses are also cited as justification for conditional forgiveness.

The Bible teaches both conditional (Matthew 18:15-17) and unconditional or unilateral forgiveness (Matthew 18:27). We can not single out one or two verses and make them the sum total of biblical forgiveness. The most important component in either is the heart. God is concerned about your heart attitude regarding forgiveness. Forgiveness must be granted freely from the heart!

The Bible is comprehensive and contains everything we need for life and godliness. The Bible has the answer for every situation we will face in the fallen world in which we live. God's expectation is that we, as His children, submit ourselves to the whole counsel of His Word.

As I stated earlier, forgiveness is a spiritual act and cannot be done in the flesh. Our sinful flesh does not want to forgive. When someone inflicts hurt and pain on us, our gut response is to do the same to them and worse if we can get away with it. Our heart is deceptive and desperately wicked (Jeremiah 17:9). The enemy of our soul lies and distorts the Word of God and uses it to lead us into disobedience and rebellion against God.

We must be extremely cautious of pursuing a course of action regarding forgiveness or any other Christian doctrine that lines up with the desires of our sinful flesh. To withhold forgiveness only because it was not asked, satisfies our sinful flesh.

> **"Our Father who is in Heaven,**
> **Hallowed be Your name,**
> **Your kingdom come.**

**Your will be done on earth as it is in Heaven.
Give us this day our daily bread.**
And forgive us our debts as we also have forgiven our debtors.
**And do not lead us into temptation but deliver us from evil.
For Yours is the kingdom and the power and the glory forever, Amen."
Matthew 6:10-13**

I want to close our study with some of the consequences of unforgiveness. This is not an exhaustive list. I have left space for you to add to the list. On the lines provided, what consequences of unforgiveness are you aware of or have experienced?

CONSEQUENCES OF UNFORGIVENESS

Unforgiveness angers God (Matthew 18:34).
Unforgiveness causes you to keep account of a wrong suffered (I Corinthians 13:5).
Unforgiveness prevents your prayers from being heard (Psalm 66:18).
Unforgiveness gives Satan an opportunity to take advantage of you (Ephesians 4:26-27).
Unforgiveness hinders spiritual growth and usefulness to God (Ephesians 4:27).
Unforgiveness demonstrates you have not received forgiveness for your sins (Matt. 6:15).

_____
_____
_____
_____
_____
_____
_____
_____
_____
_____
_____
_____

We do more dishonor to God in a day than everybody does to us in a lifetime!
– John Piper

GREAT GOD,

In public and private, in sanctuary and home,
may my life be steeped in prayer,
filled with the spirit of grace and supplication,
each prayer perfumed with the incense of atoning blood.
Help me, defend me, until from praying ground
I pass to the realm of unceasing praise.

Urged by my need,
Invited by thy promises,
Called by thy Spirit,
I enter thy presence, worshiping thee with godly fear
awed by thy majesty, greatness, glory, but encouraged by thy love,
I am all poverty as well as all guilt,
having nothing of my own with which to repay thee,
but I bring Jesus to thee in the arms of faith,
pleading his righteousness to offset my iniquities,
rejoicing that he will weigh down the scales for me,
and satisfy thy justice,
I bless thee that great sin draws out great grace,
that, although the lest sin deserves infinite punishment
because done against an infinite God,
yet there is mercy for me,
for where guilt is most terrible
there thy mercy in Christ is most free and deep.

Bless me by revealing to me more of His saving merits,
by causing thy goodness to pass before me,
by speaking peace to my contrite heart;
strengthen me to give thee no rest
until Christ shall reign supreme within me,
in every thought word, and deed,
in a faith that purifies the heart,
overcomes the world, works by love,
fastens me to thee, and ever clings to the cross.

– The Valley of Vision
Page 148

PERSONAL REFLECTIONS

THE TEN VIRGINS

THE TEN VIRGINS

(MATTHEW 25:1-13)

"Then the kingdom of heaven will be comparable to ten virgins, who took their lamps and went out to meet the bridegroom. Five of them were foolish, and five were prudent. For when the foolish took their lamps, they took no oil with them, but the prudent took oil in flasks along with their lamps. Now while the bridegroom was delaying, they all got drowsy and began to sleep. But at midnight there was a shout, 'Behold, the bridegroom! Come out to meet him.' Then all those virgins rose and trimmed their lamps. The foolish said to the prudent, 'Give us some of your oil, for our lamps are going out.' But the prudent answered, 'No, there will not be enough for us and you too; go instead to the dealers and buy some for yourselves.' And while they were going away to make the purchase, the bridegroom came, and those who were ready went in with him to the wedding feast; and the door was shut. Later the other virgins also came, saying, 'Lord, lord, open up for us.' But he answered, 'Truly I say to you, I do not know you.' Be on the alert then, for you do not know the day nor the hour."

THE TEN VIRGINS
Are You Ready To Meet The Bridegroom?

Theme: Watchfulness

Scripture: Matthew 25:1-13

Occasion: The disciples asked Jesus to tell them what would happen signaling the end of the age and His return to set up His kingdom.

Overview: Jesus explained what the kingdom of heaven would be compared to by telling the disciples a parable about ten virgins. The ten virgins had some similarities but Jesus used the differences in five of the virgins to warn His disciples, and you and me, to be prepared and ready for His imminent return.

Heart Preparation: "Make me know Your ways, O Lord; teach me Your paths. Lead me in Your truth and teach me, for You are the God of my salvation; for You I wait all the day" (Psalm 25:4-5).

THE TEN VIRGINS
Are You Ready To Meet The Bridegroom?

When you think about it, we spend a lot of time preparing for upcoming events: a wedding, the birth of a baby, moving into a new house, school tuition, a medical procedure, just to name a few. It seems there is always something for which we must prepare. However, there is no greater or more critical event in human history for which to prepare than the coming of the Lord Jesus Christ.

The Old Testament Prophets prophesied about it; the New Testament authors wrote about it; and Jesus Himself described it on numerous occasions. On one such occasion, Jesus encouraged His disciples with the following words:

> **"Be dressed in readiness, and keep your lamps lit.**
> **Be like men who are waiting for their master**
> **When he returns from the wedding feast,**
> **So that they may immediately open the door to him when he comes and knocks.**
> **Blessed are those slaves**
> **Whom the master will find on the alert when he comes;**
> **Truly I say to you, that he will gird himself to serve,**
> **And have them recline at the table, and will come up and wait on them.**
> **Whether he comes in the second watch, or even in the third,**
> **And finds them so, blessed are those slaves."**
> **Luke 12:35-38**

Have you thought about the fact that even our Lord and Savior Jesus Christ is preparing for an event? He is preparing for the time when He will come again and receive His bride (the church) unto Himself.

The chorus of one of my favorite hymns growing up has these words,

> "Coming again, coming again; may be morning, may be noon,
> may be evening and may be soon. Coming again, coming again;
> O what a wonderful day it will be, Jesus is coming again!"

Amen! It will be a wonderful day. It will be a glorious day. It will be a joyous occasion that, "eye has not seen and ear has not heard, and which have not entered the heart of man, all that God has prepared for those who love Him" (I Corinthians 2:9).

However, for some, it will not be wonderful. For some, the day of Christ' return will find them facing the consequences of being unprepared to meet Him.

Our study of the Parable of the Ten Virgins is about being prepared for the return of Jesus Christ. The first time Jesus came, He came as a baby in a manger to give His life as a ransom and to bring salvation to the lost. According to Acts 1:7, "it is not for us to know times and epochs which the Father has fixed by His own authority." However, we do know that the next time Jesus comes, He will come to judge and to rule, to separate and to reward. He will come suddenly and He will come unexpectedly (Matthew 24:42-44). Will you be ready to meet Him?

Before we study the parable, let's take a look at what the Bible teaches about the coming of our Savior. Look up the following verses and jot down what you learn about Jesus and His *first* coming.

1. **Isaiah 7:14**

   _____
   _____
   _____

2. **Isaiah 9:6**

   _____
   _____
   _____

3. **Isaiah 53:1-12**

   _____
   _____
   _____
   _____
   _____
   _____
   _____

4. **John 1:29**

   _____
   _____
   _____

The Ten Virgins

5. **Romans 8:3**

   _____
   _____
   _____

6. **Philippians 2:5-8**

   _____
   _____
   _____

Next, look up the following verses and jot down what you learn about Jesus and His *second* coming.

7. **Matthew 24:37-44**

   _____
   _____
   _____

8. **I Thessalonians 5:1-3**

   _____
   _____
   _____

9. **Revelation 1:7**

   _____
   _____
   _____

10. **Revelation 19:11-16**

    _____
    _____
    _____

11. Did you notice in Revelation 19:11-16 the names of our coming Savior? "**Faithful and True**," "**The Word of God**," and "**King of Kings and Lord of Lords**." What do these names mean to you as a daughter of the King?

    _____
    _____
    _____

With these truths in mind let us turn to the Parable of the Ten Virgins and consider what it teaches about being prepared for the return of Christ. Read **Matthew 25:1-13**.

> **"Then the kingdom of heaven will be comparable to ten virgins,**
> **Who took their lamps and went out to meet the bridegroom."**
> **Matthew 25:1**

Jesus used the illustration of a Jewish wedding to teach and to warn the disciples about being ready for His return.

Jewish weddings of that day were celebrated quite differently than our western culture weddings. One unique difference was that wedding ceremonies began in the late evening, with celebrations customarily lasting several days.

It was also customary for the groom and his friends (groomsmen), along with musicians, singers, and individuals carrying oil-fueled lamps to proceed to the home of the bride for the commencement of the celebrations. Various ceremonies were conducted at her home, which could possibly explain the delay of the bridegroom in the parable. Often, ceremonies tended to go longer than expected.

Once the ceremonies concluded at the bride's house, the couple, with an entourage of attendants and friends, would form a procession and make their way back through the streets to the home of the bridegroom. The evening activities, which were for invited guests only, would culminate with a marriage feast at the home of the bridegroom. Once inside, the door would be shut and no one else would be allowed to enter.

You can understand why there was a need for extra oil. It would be especially necessary for those waiting for the procession to get back to the bridegroom's house.

The ten virgins would have been among those waiting for the procession to approach the home of the bridegroom. With the announcement of his coming, they would be awakened from their sleep, quickly light their lamps and head out to meet the long awaited bridegroom.

Weddings are some of my all time favorite events. I have attended numerous weddings over the years that ranged in size from small and intimate to very large. However, I have never attended a wedding that began at midnight, nor one with half of the bridesmaids absent.

The Ten Virgins

What would you do if you were told that half of your bridesmaids were unprepared to participate in your wedding? What would you do if the ushers closed the doors and half of your bridesmaids had not arrived but were on their way to another part of town?

When Solomon said "there is a time for every event under heaven"(Ecclesiastes 3:1), it was certainly true of weddings.

There is a time to order the cake.
There is a time to purchase the dress.
There is a time to select the bridesmaids.
There is a time to shop for the perfect shoes.
There is a time to reserve the venue and there is a time for the wedding to begin.

In the parable, the bridegroom's arrival signaled the time for the marriage feast to begin and all invited guests were to be ready. However, five of the virgins were foolish.

> **"Five of them were foolish, and five were prudent.**
> **For when the foolish took their lamps, they took no oil with them**
> **But the prudent took oil in flasks along with their lamps."**
> **Matthew 25:2-4**

The fact that some of the virgins were wise and some were foolish should not be shocking. Neighborhoods, communities, churches and even families are also comprised of both the wise and the foolish.

12. Look up **Proverbs 13:16** and write what it says about the character of the wise and the foolish.

_____
_____

Wisdom and folly are familiar themes throughout Scripture. We are urged to choose the way of wisdom and warned to run from folly. Let's look at a few more Scriptures.

13. **Read Psalm 14:1** and write it on the lines below.

_____
_____
_____

Mysteries of the Kingdom Revealed

14. How does Solomon describe the difference between the wise and the foolish in **Ecclesiastes 7:4?**
    _____
    _____
    _____

15. According to **Proverbs 27:12**, what marks a foolish person?
    _____
    _____
    _____

16. According to **Proverbs 1:1-5**, how does wisdom serve those who heed it?
    _____
    _____
    _____

17. **Read Proverbs 1:7** and write it on the lines below.
    _____
    _____
    _____

Next, let's spend some time in Proverbs 8 and 9. You will immediately notice that both wisdom and folly are personified as women. Read **Proverbs 8:1-9** and answer the following questions.

18. From where does wisdom call and what is the meaning?
    _____
    _____
    _____

19. To whom does wisdom call?
    _____
    _____

20. What does wisdom say to the ones called?
    _____
    _____

21. How does wisdom describe herself in **Proverbs 8:12, 14, 20**?
    _____
    _____

22. Summarize wisdom's appeal in **Proverbs 8:32-36**.

_____
_____

COMPARE AND CONTRAST

PROVERBS 9:1-6 (Wise Woman)	PROVERBS 9:13-18 (Foolish Woman)
1Wisdom has built her house She has hewn out her seven pillars 2She has prepared her food, she has mixed her wine; She has also set her table; 3She has sent out her maidens, she calls from the tops of the heights of the city: 4"Whoever is naive, let him turn in here! To him who lacks understanding she says, 5Come, eat of my food and drink of the wine I have mixed. 6Forsake your folly and live. And proceed in the way of understanding"	13The woman of folly is boisterous, she is naive and knows nothing. 14She sits at the doorway of her house; on a seat by the high places of the city 15Calling to those who pass by, who are making their paths straight 16Whoever is naive, let him turn in here And to him who lacks understanding she says, 17"Stolen water is sweet; and bread eaten in secret is pleasant." 18But he does not know that the dead are there, that her guests are in the depths of Sheol.

23. From the chart above, in what ways do wisdom and folly appear to be parallel? What are the differences between the two as represented in the passage? What does wisdom promote and what does folly promote?

_____
_____
_____
_____
_____
_____

> **"Now while the bridegroom was delaying,**
> **they all got drowsy and began to sleep.**
> **But at midnight there was a shout,**
> **'Behold, the bridegroom! Come out to meet him.'**
> **Then all those virgins rose and trimmed their lamps."**
> **Matthew 25:5-7**

Until the bridegroom arrived, all ten virgins outwardly appeared to be prepared to meet him. There was nothing about them or their behavior that indicated a lack of readiness. Notice the unifying characteristics of the virgins:

All ten were virgins or "maidens." We would call them "bridesmaids."
All ten virgins had been invited and had responded to the invitation.
All ten virgins had their own lamp and together they were waiting to meet the bridegroom.
All ten virgins were responsible for their own lamp, no one was held accountable for another virgin's lamp.
All ten virgins fully intended and expected to participate in the marriage feast.
All ten virgins were impacted by the delay of the bridegroom as they became drowsy and slept.
All ten virgins were awakened by the arrival of the bridegroom.

> **"The foolish said to the prudent,**
> **'Give us some of your oil, for our lamps are going out.'**
> **But the prudent answered,**
> **'No, there will not be enough for us and you too;**
> **Go instead to the dealers and buy some for yourselves.'**
> **And while they were going away to make the purchase,**
> **The bridegroom came,**
> **And those who were ready went in with him to the wedding feast;**
> **And the door was shut."**
> **Matthew 25:8-10**

The wise will _act with knowledge_ and the fool will _display folly_ (Proverbs 13:16).

The five foolish virgins displayed folly when it was discovered that their lamps did not have enough oil to participate in the wedding feast.

The Ten Virgins

As the disciples listened, the Bible doesn't tell us whether or not they understood that the bridegroom represented Jesus and that the virgins represented all followers of Christ. The Bible doesn't tell us whether or not the disciples understood that some "followers" of Christ will be shut out of the kingdom because they will be unprepared to meet the bridegroom.

The five wise virgins were wise because they had prepared for the coming of the bridegroom, the single most important event. They represent true, genuine followers who long for the appearance of the Bridegroom and conduct their life with a view to His coming. When he finally arrived,

"Those who were ready went in with him to the wedding feast...."
Matthew 25:10

24. What thoughts come to mind knowing that one day Jesus (the Bridegroom) will escort you into the wedding feast with Him?

_____
_____
_____

Notice what the Apostle John said about the Marriage of the Lamb in Revelation. Read **Revelation 19:6-8.**

25. What was the "voice of a great multitude" saying?

_____
_____
_____

26. What two things had occurred that caused the eruption of praise?

_____
_____
_____

27. According to verse 8, what clothing was worn by the bride and what did it represent?

_____
_____
_____

Mysteries of the Kingdom Revealed

28. Read **Romans 13:11-14**. There are at least 6 "righteous acts" that Paul exhorts the Romans to do. Write them on the lines below.

_____
_____
_____
_____
_____

The Marriage Feast of the Lamb is for people who have received an invitation and have put on "fine linen, bright and clean" (Revelation 19:7-8).

> **"Later the other virgins also came, saying,**
> **'Lord, lord, open up for us.'**
> **But he answered, 'Truly I say to you, I do not know you.'"**
> **Matthew 25:11-12**

In New Testament Jewish culture, going out at night with a lack of oil for your lamp was no small matter and no mere oversight. It would be considered gross negligence and inexcusable.

Once the bridegroom arrived and the foolish virgins were unprepared to meet him, the lines of distinction became clear and were irrevocably drawn. "Seek the Lord while He may be found..." (Isaiah 55:6). When the foolish virgins came seeking, they found a closed door.

29. Read **Matthew 25:7-12** again. What dividing characteristics became evident when the bridegroom arrived?

_____
_____
_____
_____
_____
_____
_____

"I do not know you" are the saddest words in the parable. You may have questioned the charity of the wise virgins when they staunchly refused to share their oil. You may have been dismayed at the arrival of the bridegroom just as the foolish virgins left the scene.

However, the words "I do not know you" should leave little doubt in your mind that despite appearances, the foolish virgins were unprepared to meet the bridegroom and therefore excluded from the marriage feast.

The ending of the Parable of the Ten Virgins closely resembles the ending of another parable. Read **Luke 13:23-27**.

30. What did the people do when they found themselves on the wrong side of a closed door?

31. What reasons did they offer as justification to be allowed to enter?

32. What was the response of the "head of the house"?

The foolish virgins were foolish because they were insufficiently prepared for the coming of the bridegroom. Outwardly, they looked just like the wise virgins.
They received an invitation to a wedding feast.
They responded to the invitation.
They had a lamp.
They gathered where the wise virgins gathered.
They knew about the coming of the Bridegroom.
They even called upon his name, crying, "Lord, lord."

Ultimately what the foolish virgins needed was salvation. They lacked saving faith in the Lord Jesus Christ. Charles Spurgeon put it this way:

> "A great change has to be wrought in you, far beyond any power of yours to accomplish, ere you can go in with Christ to the marriage. You must, first of all, be <u>renewed</u> in your nature, or you will not be ready. You must be <u>washed</u> from your sins, or you will not be ready.

> You must be <u>justified</u> in Christ's righteousness, and you must <u>put on his wedding dress</u>, or else you will not be ready. You must be <u>reconciled</u> to God, you must be <u>made like</u> to God, or you will not be ready. Or, to come to the parable before us, you must have a lamp, and that lamp must be fed with heavenly oil and it must continue to burn brightly or else you will not be ready. No child of darkness can go into that place of light, you must be <u>bought out of nature's darkness</u> into God's marvelous light, or else you will never be ready to go in with Christ to the marriage, and to be forever with him."[1]

Many Bible scholars have indicated that the parable of the Ten Virgins is by far the scariest parable because it is about people in the church. It is not teaching about enemies of the cross or those who would use the cross of Christ for sordid gain. It is about people who consider themselves to be in the family of God. They are faithfully serving, church-going people who *profess* Christ but do not *possess* Christ. It is a parable about people in the church who are familiar with and associated with Christ but do not have a relationship with Christ.

There have always been those in the church who attempt to pass off as authentic that which is counterfeit. The Bible identifies them in the following way:

"This people honors Me with their lips but their heart is far away from Me."
Matthew 15:8

They hold to a "form of godliness, although they have denied its power."
II Timothy 3:5

Those with authentic faith are identified as people who will:

Examine Themselves "Test yourselves to see if you are in the faith; examine yourselves. Or do you not recognize this about yourselves, that Jesus Christ is in you – unless indeed you fail the test" (II Corinthians 13:5).

---

[1] Charles Haddon Spurgeon, "*Entrance and Exclusion*," in Metropolitan Tabernacle Pulpit, vols. 7-63 (Pasadena, Texas: Pilgrim Publications, 1976) 43:30

"Therefore brethren, be all the more diligent to make certain about His calling and choosing you for as long as you practice these things, you will never stumble" (II Peter 1:10).

Seek the Lord

"Seek the Lord while He may be found, call upon Him while He is near. Let the wicked forsake his way and the unrighteous man his thoughts; and let him return to the Lord, and He will have compassion on him, and to our God, for He will abundantly pardon" (Isaiah 55:6-7).

Desire the Word

"Like newborn babies, long for the pure milk of the Word, so that by it you may grow in respect to salvation" (I Peter 2:2).

"Your words were found and I ate them, and Your words became for me a joy and the delight of my heart for I have been called by Your name, O Lord God of hosts" (Jeremiah 15:16).

Bear Fruit

"I am the Vine and you are the branches; he who abides in Me and I in him, he bears much fruit, for apart from Me you can do nothing" (John 15:5).

"By this is My Father glorified, that you bear much fruit and so prove to be My disciples" (John 15:8).

Grow in Grace

"But grow in the grace and knowledge of our Lord and Savior Jesus Christ" (II Peter 3:18).

Practice Righteousness

"Little children, make sure no one deceives you; the one who practices righteousness is righteous, just as He is righteous . . . No one who is born of God practices sin, because His seed abides in him; and he cannot sin, because he is born of God. By this the children of God and the children of the devil are obvious: anyone who does not practice righteousness is not of God, nor the one who does not love his brother" (I John 3:7, 9-10).

Love and forgive

"We know that we have passed out of death into life, because we love the brethren. He who does not love abides in death.

Everyone who hates his brother is a murderer; and you know that no murderer has eternal life abiding in him" (I John 3:14-15).

"Whenever you stand praying, forgive, if you have anything against anyone, so that your Father who is in heaven will also forgive you your transgressions. But if you do not forgive, neither will your Father who is in heaven forgive your transgressions" (Mark 11:25-26).

**"He who testifies to these things says,
'Yes, I am coming quickly.'
Amen. Come, Lord Jesus."
Revelation 22:20**

THOU GOD OF ALL GRACE,
Thou hast given me a Saviour,
produce in me a faith to live by Him
to make Him all my desire,
all my hope,
all my glory.

May I enter Him as my refuge,
build on Him as my foundation,
walk in Him as my way,
follow Him as my guide,
conform to Him as my example,
receive His instructions as my prophet,
rely on His intercession as my high priest,
obey Him as my king.

May I never be ashamed of Him or His words,
but joyfully bear His reproach,
never displease Him by unholy or imprudent conduct,
never count it a glory if I take it patiently
when buffeted for a fault,
never make the multitude my model,
never delay when thy word invites me to advance.

May thy dear Son preserve me from this present evil world,
so that it's smiles never allure,
nor it's frowns terrify,
nor it's vices defile,
nor it's errors delude me.
May I feel that I am a stranger and a pilgrim on earth,
declaring plainly that I seek a country,
my title to it becoming daily more clear,
my meetness for it more perfect,
my foretastes of it more abundant;
and whatsoever I do may it be done in the Saviour's name.

– The Valley of Vision
Page 44

PERSONAL REFLECTIONS

THE TALENTS

THE TALENTS

(MATTHEW 25:14-30)

"For it is just like a man about to go on a journey, who called his own slaves and entrusted his possessions to them. To one he gave five talents, to another, two, and to another, one, each according to his own ability; and he went on his journey. Immediately the one who had received the five talents went and traded with them, and gained five more talents. In the same manner the one who had received the two talents gained two more. But he who received the one talent went away, and dug a hole in the ground and hid his master's money. Now after a long time the master of those slaves came and settled accounts with them. The one who had received the five talents came up and brought five more talents, saying, 'Master, you entrusted five talents to me. See, I have gained five more talents.' His master said to him, 'Well done, good and faithful slave. You were faithful with a few things, I will put you in charge of many things, enter into the joy of your master.' Also the one who had received the two talents came up and said, 'Master, you entrusted two talents to me. See, I have gained two more talents.' His master said to him, 'Well done, good and faithful slave. You were faithful with a few things, I will put you in charge of many things; enter into the joy of your master.' And the one also who had received the one talent came up and said, 'Master, I knew you to be a hard man, reaping where you did not sow and gathering where you scattered no seed. And I was afraid, and went away and hid your talent in the ground. See, you have what is yours.' But his master answered and said to him, 'You wicked, lazy slave, you knew that I reap where I did not sow and gather where I scattered no seed. Then you ought to have put my money in the bank and on my arrival I would have received my money back with interest. Therefore take away the talent from him, and give it to the one who has the ten talents.' For to everyone who has, more shall be given, and he will have an abundance; but from the one who does not have, even what he does have shall be taken away. Throw out the worthless slave into the outer darkness; in that place there will be weeping and gnashing of teeth."

THE TALENTS
It's Not About How Much You Have
But Faithfulness With What You Have

Theme: Serving While Waiting

Scripture: Matthew 25:14-30

Occasion: The disciples asked Jesus to tell them what would happen to signal the end of the age and His return to set up His kingdom.

Overview: The Parable of the Talents is one of three parables Jesus taught when asked about His second coming. The focus is on serving and using the gifts God has given for His kingdom.

Heart Preparation: "Remove the false way from me, and graciously grant me Your law. I have chosen the faithful way; I have placed Your ordinances before me. I cleave to Your testimonies; O Lord, do not put me to shame! I shall run the way of Your commandments, for You will enlarge my heart" (Psalm 119:29-32).

THE TALENTS
It's Not About How Much You Have
But Faithfulness With What You Have

Have you ever labored under the false expectations of others? Have you ever tried to live up to someone else's unrealistic thoughts and ideas of who you were to be and what you were to do? In every relationship there is the potential for unrealistic expectations. Some parents, trying to live through their children, saddle them with unrealistic expectations. Newly married couples tend to have unrealistic expectations of each other. Sometimes teachers have them of their students; citizens have them of their elected officials; parishioners have them of their pastor and pastor's wife; and friends have them of other friends. We can even have unrealistic expectations of ourselves.

Attempting to function under the false expectations of others or ourselves will inevitably result in frustration and failure.

However, as believers we can be confident that God does not have false expectations of us. God's expectations of us are commensurate with who we are. They are rooted in the opportunities He orchestrates according to His sovereign will and plan for our life, and the gifts and abilities He gives us.

Moses, Solomon, and Paul were each given different and unique opportunities by God. God spoke "mouth to mouth" with Moses, calling him through a burning bush to lead the Israelites from captivity in Egypt to salvation in the Promised Land (Numbers 12:8; Exodus 3:1-4:31).

Solomon was the wisest man on earth, second only to Jesus. God appeared to Solomon in a dream in which He gave him the opportunity to make a request for himself. Solomon asked for wisdom. He said, "Give Your servant an understanding heart to judge Your people to discern between good and evil..." (1 Kings 3:7-14).

Paul met Jesus Christ on his way to persecute and murder Christians. After a light from heaven shown around him, Paul fell to the ground and Jesus said, "Saul, Saul, why are you persecuting Me" (Acts 9:4)? Later on the Lord told Ananias that Saul was "a chosen instrument of Mine, to bear My name before the Gentiles and kings and the sons of Israel; for I will show him how much he must suffer for My name's sake" (Acts 9: 4, 15-16).

Esther, Mary the mother of Jesus, and countless other women were given different and unique opportunities by God. Think about the opportunity given to Mary the mother of Jesus. The angel Gabriel told Mary, "Behold you will conceive in your womb and bear a son, and you shall name Him Jesus" (Luke 1:31). Mary could not understand how she would conceive given the fact that she was a virgin. However she responded to Gabriel and said, "Behold, the bond slave of the Lord; may it be done to me according to your word" (Luke 1:38). There could only be one mother of Jesus and God gave that opportunity to Mary.

God is not mentioned in her story, though, Esther was given the opportunity by God to save the Jewish people from annihilation. Sternly warning Esther not to remain silent, Mordecai said, "And who knows whether you have not attained royalty for such a time as this" (Esther 4:14)? Esther boldly and confidently stated, "I will go in to the king, which is not according to the law; and if I perish, I perish" (Esther 4:16).

God's expectations of all those mentioned above were vastly different, yet orchestrated according to His sovereign will and plan for their life. The same is true of you and me.

Although we have all been created equal, no individual is more human than another, we are not all the same. We do not all have the same abilities or opportunities. This is according to God's perfect and holy design. Notice what Paul said in Romans:

> **"On the contrary, who are you, O man, who answers back to God?**
> **The thing molded will not say to the molder,**
> **'Why did you make me like this,' will it?**
> **Or does not the potter have a right over the clay,**
> **To make from the same lump one vessel for honorable use**
> **And another for common use?"**
> **Romans 9:20-21**

As His "vessel," God alone determines how your life will be utilized; He has the right to dispose of your life the way He chooses. You have been given opportunities and responsibilities by God for His kingdom purposes. His expectation is that, through faithful obedience and service, He will receive a maximum return on what He has given to you. A total commitment of yourself to the opportunities and responsibilities is required in order to fulfill His expectation of you.

With these things in mind, let's begin our study of The Parable of the Talents.

The disciples asked Jesus a question about the sign of His coming and "the end of the age" (Matthew 24:3). He answered their question in the form of three parables that contain similar messages (Matthew 25:1-46). If the disciples could not understand the message from the Parable of the Ten Virgins, perhaps they would understand it from the

Parable of the Talents, or perhaps the Parable of the Sheep and the Goats (Matthew 25:31-46) would resonate with them.

Jesus told the disciples numerous times that no one would know the day nor the hour when the Son of Man comes. They were to focus not on "when," but on being ready for His return (Matthew 24:36, 43, 44, 50; 25:13). However, Jesus identified some of the signs leading up to the end of the age and His second coming.

1. Read **Matthew 24:5-14.** What signs did Jesus tell the disciples to expect when the end drew near?

2. Are you seeing some of these signs today? If so, which ones? How is your walk with the Lord impacted as a result of these signs?

The Parable of the Talents is a seamless continuation of Jesus' exhortation about how the disciples should conduct themselves until His return. They were to be watchful and ready while working, serving and using the opportunities God gave them to further His kingdom.

> **"For it is just like a man about to go on a journey,**
> **Who called his own slaves and entrusted his possessions to them.**
> **To one he gave five talents, to another, two, and to another, one,**
> **Each according to his own ability; and he went on his journey."**
> **Matthew 25:14-15**

Jesus used the same familiar theme of a master leaving on a journey and returning after a long time. The master gathered three of his servants and gave them each a portion of his wealth prior to his departure. What the servants did with what was entrusted to them is the point of the parable.

First, notice the phrase "his own slaves" in Matthew 25:14. The word for "slave" is *doulos*[1] and does not mean someone uneducated or of lower class but someone who was owned by another and could not live his life however he pleased. The slaves depicted in the parable were highly skilled and trained individuals who had a good mind for business. They were very capable of successfully using the talent(s) they were given.

Keep in mind that the word "talent" does not refer to human natural ability, but rather was a monetary weight of approximately 60 to 90 pounds. "The value of a talent was equivalent to 6000 days' wages of a day laborer (roughly twenty years' work)."[2]

It is clear that the master of the slaves was enormously wealthy and gave his servants a large sum of his money. Although the last servant was given only one talent, it was still a substantial amount of money.

3. According to Matthew 25:15, how did the master decide who would get what amount?

_____

_____

"Talents" represent the various opportunities and responsibilities given to you by the Lord for His kingdom. We may think that "talents" are one entity of life: the ministries in our local church, the Bible study we conduct in our home or the missionaries we financially support. However, "talents" encompass all of life. Notice how one theologian explains it:

> "Anything whereby we may glorify God is a talent. Our gifts, our influence, our money, our knowledge, our health, our strength, our time, our senses, our reason, our intellect, our memory, our affections, our privileges as members of Christ's Church, our advantages as possessors of the Bible–all, all are talents. Whence came these things? What hand bestowed them? Why are we what we are? Why are we not the worms that crawl on the earth? There is only one answer to these

---

[1] Verlyn D. Verbrugge. *The NIV Theological Dictionary of New Testament Words*, (Zondervan Publishing House, Grand Rapids MI, 2000), 350.

[2] Klyne R. Snodgrass. *Stories With Intent*; Wm. B. Eerdmans Publishing Co., Grand Rapids/Cambridge. 528

questions. All that we have is a loan from God. We are God's stewards. We are God's debtors. Let this thought sink deeply into our hearts."³

The entirety of your life are the opportunities and responsibilities given to you for kingdom purposes. They are your "talents."

4. Look up the following verses and jot down how each woman used her "talents" (opportunities) for the kingdom of God?

    A.   **Jochebed (Exodus 2:1-10)**

    B.   **Rahab (Joshua 2:1-21)**

    C.   **Deborah (Judges 4:1-10)**

    D.   Mary, Joanna and Susanna (Luke 8:1-3)

    E.   King Lemuel's Mother (Proverbs 31:1-31)

    F.   Anna (Luke 2:36-38)

---

[3] https://scripturethoughts.wordpress.com/2011/05/21/j-c-ryle-*our-talent-on-loan-from-god*/

G. **The Samaritan Woman (John 4:28-42)**

H. **Dorcas (Acts 9:36-42)**

I. **Priscilla (Acts 18:24-38)**

J. **Phoebe (Romans 16:1-2)**

5. Think about the women you know who have used the opportunities and responsibilities God gave them for His kingdom. Did any of them impact your life personally? If so, write one or two names on the lines below and briefly explain how your life was impacted by their faithfulness.

Second, notice there were no protest by the slaves because of the amounts received. The one who received two talents did not complain that his fellow slave received three more than him. The one-talent slave did not complain that he was given the least amount of the group. No one questioned the master as to why he did not entrust them with more. Each slave took what was given and went his way.

That was not the scene in an earlier parable Jesus taught. Rather than accepting what was given, some of the workers complained to their employer.

Read **Matthew 20:1-16**. "The Parable of the Workers In The Vineyard."

The Talents

6. What was the complaint of "those hired first"?

___

7. How did the landowner answer their complaint?

___

Some of the individuals worked only an hour whereas others worked the majority of the day. Each worker received the same amount as his fellow worker received. There was no variance. The individuals who worked the longest hours did not get a penny more than the individuals who came on the job literally in the eleventh hour. From the parable, we learn an important lesson about the kingdom of God. We learn that everyone who gets into the kingdom comes in equally. Everyone is <u>equal</u> at the foot of the cross. Everyone is <u>equal</u> in that we all must enter through the cleansing blood of Jesus Christ.

8. How does the Bible describe our equal standing coming into the kingdom of God according to the following verses?

    A. **Romans 6:17-19**

___

    B. **Ephesians 2:1-6**

___

    C. **Colossians 1:19-22**

___

Salvation is available and free to all (Romans 6:23). No one gets in on their own merit or by their own ingenuity. No one gets more of the kingdom because they were saved longer than another person. Everyone who receives Christ as Lord and Savior receives the same gift: eternal life. This is why the thief on the cross of whom Jesus said, "This day you will be with me in Paradise" (Luke 23:43) will receive just as much of the kingdom of

Mysteries of the Kingdom Revealed

God as the prophetess Anna who lived to be eighty-four and "never left the temple, serving night and day with fastings and prayers" (Luke 2:37). The responsibilities and rewards they receive in the kingdom will vary significantly. However, both will experience the kingdom. The Parable of the Talents demonstrates that after salvation has taken place, we are not all the same in regards to the opportunities and responsibilities given. Each of us differ in "talents" and the extent to which they are used.

9. How did Paul explain this truth in the following verse?

I Corinthians 12:12-25

_____
_____
_____
_____

10. Read again **I Corinthians 12:18** and write it on the lines below.

_____
_____
_____
_____

In light of our study, the verse could read as follows:
    But now God has given *talents* to all members, each one of
    them in the kingdom, just as *He* desired!

Third, notice that two of the servants effectively used what was given and the master's money increased.

> **"Immediately the one who had received the five talents**
> **went and traded with them,**
> **and gained five more talents.**
> **In the same manner the one who had received the two talents**
> **gained two more."**
> **Matthew 25:16-17**

The word "immediately" carries the ideas of eagerness, joy and anticipation of a positive outcome. "The stress is on the vigor with which the two faithful servants undertook the responsibility that had been given them. Not knowing how much time they would have, they quickly set to work, trading and investing."[4] As a result, they each received the same commendation and reward, demonstrating that the reward was based not on the amount accumulated but on faithfulness (Matthew 25:20-23).

Sadly, the last servant completely disrupted the flow of events. Rather than excitement and joy for the opportunity to increase his master's wealth, excuses and lies filled his mouth. Instead of faithful labor on behalf of the master, the slave buried his talent and returned it just as it was given.

It was not uncommon to bury money in ancient times according to Joshua 7:19-21 and Matthew 13:44. However, the slave did not bury the money because he intended to do something with it later.

11. Read **Matthew 25:24-25**. What reasons (lies) did the slave give for burying his master's money?

_____

_____

_____

_____

All throughout scripture, people have attempted to explain sinful behavior with excuses and accusations. It began in the garden with the first man and woman. When Adam was confronted by God to answer for his sinful behavior, the excuse was, "The woman whom You gave to be with me..." (Genesis 3:12). The woman, following in the same pattern, stated that the serpent had caused her to take a bite of the forbidden fruit (Genesis 3:13). God did not accept it then, nor will He ever accept our attempts to excuse sin.

Perhaps the slave thought he had an ironclad excuse. Just like Adam blamed God for his sinful behavior, the slave blamed his master, essentially saying, "You're the reason the money sat buried in the ground." He had a faulty view of his master.

The master represents God the Father. The three slaves represent professing Christians. The "talent" represents responsibilities and opportunities given by God. Like the first two slaves, some who profess to be Christians are faithfully serving the Lord with the "talents" they have received. However, there are others who like the third slave have buried their "talent." They identify with Christ, but do not read His Word regularly. They identify with Christ but do not put into practice what His Word says. They identify with Christ but pursue their own agenda rather than serving the body of Christ faithfully. They bury their talent.

---

[4] John MacArthur. *Parables*; Thomas Nelson Publishing Co., Nashville, TN 136

The Psalmist beautifully articulates the right view we should have of God. Take a few moments to read and meditate on **Psalm 145:8-20**.

12. What an incredibly wonderful God we serve. How did God speak to you through this Psalm? How does knowing these truths help you serve Christ more vigorously?

    _____
    _____
    _____
    _____
    _____
    _____
    _____
    _____
    _____

Read again **Psalm 145:20** and take note of what is said about the wicked.

13. Turning back to the Parable of the Talents, how did the master respond to the false allegations of the slave (Matthew 25:26-30)?

    _____
    _____
    _____
    _____
    _____
    _____

14. Laziness is another subject that Solomon spends a lot of time talking about in the book of Proverbs. Look up the following verses and write down what you learn about laziness.

    A. **Proverbs 6:6-11**

    _____
    _____

    B. **Proverbs 10:4, 26**

    _____
    _____

    C. **Proverbs 12:27**

    _____
    _____

D. **Proverbs 15:19**

_____

_____

E. **Proverbs 18:9**

_____

_____

F. **Proverbs 20:4**

_____

_____

G. **Proverbs 21:25**

_____

_____

15. Besides the fact of being wicked and worthless, what else according to **Proverbs 6:12** characterizes the lazy person?

_____

_____

When people "walk with a false mouth," they have abandoned truth. It is second nature for them to devise and imagine unreal circumstances and situations about themselves, about others, and about the world in general. They live in a false narrative of their own making in order to mask their sinful heart attitude. What is created in their mind becomes justification for their actions. (Notice from the chart below how the last slave resembled the sluggard in Proverbs).

FALSE NARRATIVE	CORRESPONDING ACTIONS
The Slave: "I knew you to be a hard man, reaping where you did not sow and gathering where you scattered no seed" (Matthew 25:24).	"And I was afraid and went away and hid your talent in the ground" (Matthew 25:25).
The Sluggard: "There is a lion in the road! A lion is in the open square" (Proverbs 26:13).	"As the door turns on its hinges, so does the sluggard on his bed" (Proverbs 26:14).

Mysteries of the Kingdom Revealed

If you are forced to work for a man who is cruel and hard, and who takes what does not belong to him, it makes sense to be fearful. It makes sense to keep his money tucked away someplace safe so you can present it to him untouched when he asks for it. Just as it makes sense to turn over and remain in bed rather than going out to work when there's a lion in the street. The problem is that none of it was true. The reality of the matter is that the sluggard was called a sluggard because that's what he was. He was lazy. Rather than change his character and become a wise, productive citizen, he chose to lie to himself and act upon the lies. According to Proverbs 26:16, the sluggard refuses to listen to reason and continues in his own faulty way of thinking.

The problem with the one-talent slave was that he lived in a false narrative of his own making. He devised multiple lies about his master in order to mask his laziness. He wasted his "talent" and justified his actions by blaming his master.

Earlier we looked at women who the Bible highlighted for their faithful use of their "talent." They used their opportunities and responsibilities for the kingdom of God. But like the last slave, there were also women who misused and wasted their "talent."

16. Look up the following verses and briefly explain how each woman wasted her opportunities and responsibilities and negatively impacted the kingdom of God.

> A. **Eve (Genesis 3:1-6)**
>
> _____
> _____
> _____
>
> B. **Peninnah (I Samuel 1:1-23)**
>
> _____
> _____
> _____
>
> C. **Michal (II Samuel 6:15-23)**
>
> _____
> _____
> _____
>
> D. **Athaliah (II Chronicles 22:1-12)**
>
> _____
> _____
> _____
> _____

E. **Gomer (Hosea 1:1-11; 2:1-7)**

F. **Herodias (Matthew 14:3-12)**

G. **Sapphira (Acts 5:1-11)**

H. **Jezebel (Revelation 2:20)**

What a horrendous resume of women who did great harm to the people of God. They chose the way of destruction and were severely judged for their sinful actions.

We know that the enemy's chief end in life is to steal, kill, and destroy (John 10:10). Solomon said, "He also who is slack in his work is brother to him who destroys" (Proverbs 18:9). Perhaps unintentionally, the last slave engaged in the destruction of his own life. He destroyed his **position**. He was no longer viewed as the master's slave but a "worthless slave." He destroyed his **reputation**. He was called wicked and lazy. He destroyed his **relationships**. He was not welcomed into the joy of his master with his fellow slaves. He destroyed his **future**. The master assigned him to a place of "outer darkness; in that place there will be weeping and gnashing of teeth" (Matthew 25:30). In closing,

17. What can women of God do to safeguard themselves from wasting their "talent" and negatively impacting the kingdom of God?

Mysteries of the Kingdom Revealed

18. How do sinful actions and attitudes such as gossip, envy, jealousy and slander negatively impact the kingdom of God?

_____

By his own actions the slave proved himself to be unworthy of the master's blessing and deserving of the master's condemnation. He was eternally judged for wasting his "talent."

> "To accept the kingdom and its salvation is to accept a trust.
> It enlists one as an agent on behalf of the kingdom,
> and all those so enlisted will be rewarded or judged
> in terms of their faithfulness to their task."[5]

**"As each one has received a special gift,
employ it in serving one another as good stewards of the manifold grace of God."
I Peter 4:10**

_____

[5] Klyne R. Snodgrass. *Stories With Intent*; Wm. B. Eerdmans Publishing Co., Grand Rapids/Cambridge. 542

The Talents

BENIGN LORD,
I praise thee continually
for permission to approach thy throne of grace,
and to spread my wants and desires before thee.
I am not worthy of thy blessings and mercies
for I am far gone from original righteousness;
My depraved nature reveals itself in disobedience and rebellion;
My early days discovered in me discontent, pride, envy, revenge.
Remember not the sins of my youth,
nor the multiplied transgressions of later years,
my failure to improve time and talents,
my abuse of mercies and means,
my wasted sabbaths,
my perverted seasons of grace,
my long neglect of thy great salvation,
my disregard of the friend of sinners.
While I confess my guilt,
help me to feel it deeply,
with self-abhorrence and self-despair,
yet to remember there is hope in thee,
and to see the Lamb that takes away sin.
Through him may I return to thee,
listen to thee, trust in thee, delight in thy law, obey thee,
be upheld by thee.
Preserve my understanding from error,
my affections from love of idols,
my lips from speaking guile,
my conduct from stain of vice,
my character from appearance of evil,
that I may be harmless, blameless,
rebukeless, exemplary, useful,
light-giving, prudent, zealous
for thy glory and the good of my fellow-men.

– The Valley of Vision
Page 145

PERSONAL REFLECTIONS

THE UNJUST JUDGE

THE UNJUST JUDGE

(LUKE 18:1-8)

"Now He was telling them a parable to show that at all times they ought to pray and not to lose heart, saying, 'In a certain city there was a judge who did not fear God and did not respect man.' There was a widow in that city, and she kept coming to him, saying, 'Give me legal protection from my opponent.'

For a while he was unwilling; but afterward he said to himself, 'Even though I do not fear God nor respect man, yet because this widow bothers me, I will give her legal protection, otherwise by continually coming she will wear me out.'

And the Lord said, 'Hear what the unrighteous judge said; now, will not God bring about justice for His elect who cry to Him day and night, and will He delay long over them? I tell you that He will bring about justice for them quickly. However, when the Son of Man comes, will He find faith on the earth?'"

THE UNJUST JUDGE
Pray Until You Pray

Theme: Perseverance in prayer

Scripture: Luke 18:1-8

Occasion: Jesus wanted to teach His disciples a lesson about prayer.

Overview: Jesus had just completed a lengthy discussion on the kingdom of God. Some of the Pharisees questioned Him as to when the kingdom of God was coming. He spoke in detail reminding them of the "days of Noah" and the "days of Lot" and how the people were unprepared for the calamities that took place. Jesus indicated that it would be the same "on the day that the Son of Man is revealed" (Luke 17:30). Turning to His disciples, He spoke a parable on persistence in prayer.

Heart Preparation: "As for me, I will call upon God, and the Lord shall save me. Evening and morning and at noon I will pray, and cry aloud, and He shall hear my voice" (Psalm 55:16-17 NKJV).

THE UNJUST JUDGE
Pray Until You Pray

"Justice is not something God has. Justice is something that God is."
– A.W. Tozer

I can count on one hand the number of times I have been in a courtroom. I know that regardless of the reason one would find themselves in a courtroom, three things are expected. A judge will emerge, a case will be heard, and justice will be executed according to the law.

There are two kinds of judges spoken of in the Bible, those who ruled according to justice and those who ruled by expediency. In the Old Testament, Samuel was a righteous judge who ruled according to justice (I Samuel 7:2-17). However, in the New Testament, Pontius Pilate proved to be an unrighteous judge. After declaring he had found no fault in the Lord Jesus, he reneged due to public pressure, and gave permission to have Him crucified (John 18:38–19:16). Our Lord and Savior Jesus Christ once stood before an unjust judge.

The Old Testament was clear about the very serious role and responsibilities of a judge. A judge was expected to "judge the people with righteous judgment" (Deuteronomy 16:18). Justice and only justice was to be pursued by every judge appointed to the bench according to Deuteronomy 16:20.
Look up **II Chronicles 19:4-7**.

1. Describe the job description of a judge as communicated by King Jehoshaphat.

   _____
   _____
   _____
   _____
   _____

As we study the parable, keep in mind that Jesus communicated the important spiritual virtue of persistence in prayer through the flagrant actions of a corrupt judge.

"Now He was telling them a parable
to show that at all times they ought to pray and not to lose heart."
Luke 18:1

The Greek word πάντοτε (*pantote*) is translated "at all times." It means ever and always.[1] It is to pray at any point, on any occasion, under any circumstance and on any account. It is to pray repeatedly. The idea is of returning time and again.

The One who faithfully answers prayer longs for and desires the prayers of His children. Think about that for a moment! The Savior of your soul wants to hear what you have to say. He wants to listen to you speak. He wants to hear about what's on your mind, your desires and your plans (Proverbs 16:9). He wants to hear about what's troubling you and the concerns of your heart (Psalm 138:8).

He wants you to cast all of your cares upon Him, again and again (I Peter 5:7). The Greek word ἐπιρρίπτω (*epiripto*) translated "cast" in I Peter 5:7, means to throw upon.[2] It is the idea of giving up to God, or transference. It is to transfer the cares and anxieties from your hands into God's all powerful and loving hands. He is ready and waiting to take on each and every one!

However, because we are "but flesh" (Psalm 78:39), we have the tendency to become discouraged and lose heart (Luke 18:1). When we lose heart, we give up and quit. The Greek word ἐγκακεω (*egkakeo*) translated "give up" means to become tired, weary, and to lack courage.[3] It is the idea of being depleted of motivation.

2. What promises does God give in **Isaiah 40:31** to those who, rather than despairing and giving up, choose to wait on Him?

_____
_____
_____
_____
_____
_____

Before we continue, let's take a sidebar and consider the things that kill our motivation to pray. Jesus said, "at <u>all</u> times they ought to pray and not to lose heart" (Luke 18:1). However, there is a devastating connection between prayer and losing heart especially when our prayers seem to be left unheard. Our sinful flesh does not want to pray and

---

[1] *Strong's Exhaustive Concordance of the Bible*, Nashville, TN: Abingdon Publishers, 1980, 54 (Greek Dictionary of the New Testament, #3842).

[2] Ibid, 31.

[3] Ibid, 26.

certainly not often. Over time the desire to pray is replaced with weariness and a lack of motivation, resulting in fewer times of prayer or no prayer.

3. Below are five "prayer motivation killers." Explain how each one could cause a woman to lose heart, give up, and quit praying altogether.

PRAYER MOTIVATION KILLERS

A. **Faulty view of God**

_____
_____
_____
_____

B. **Comparing your situation to others**

_____
_____
_____
_____

C. **Worry and frustration**

_____
_____
_____
_____

D. **Discontentment**

_____
_____
_____
_____

E. **Anger**

_____
_____
_____
_____

4. Choose one from the list above and jot down how you would encourage a girlfriend struggling in that area.

_____
_____
_____
_____
_____
_____

> "... saying, in a certain city there was a judge
> who did not fear God and did not respect man."
> **Luke 18:2**

The unjust judge was totally and completely wicked. "No fear of God" put him in a category worse than a demon. Scripture tells us that the demons "believe and shudder" (James 2:19). Just the very thought of God on the mind of a demon causes him to have tremors.

A judge overseeing and ruling cases who has no fear of God and no respect for man, will execute heinous judgments. It is utterly shameful that egregious cases such as Roe v. Wade and Obergefell v. Hodges, make up part of the history of the highest court of our land, The Supreme Court of the United States of America. Men and women appointed to the bench of the Supreme Court have shook their wretched fists in the face of God concerning human life. Who would have ever imagined that those sworn to protect the sanctity of life would pass a landmark ruling legalizing the murder of innocent babies? Who would have imagined that a day and time would come in which two people of the same-sex could legally form a union that is to be recognized as a marital union? In the summer of 2015, marriage was redefined in our country with the unprecedented ruling of Obergefell v. Hodges. It was yet another example of Justices evidencing no fear of God and no regard for human life.

However, our focus in this lesson is ultimately on prayer and persistence in it. One example of the kind of prayer God expects of His people is found in Paul's letter to Timothy.

Turn to **I Timothy 2:1-4** and answer the questions on the following page.

5. *What* 4 things does Paul urge of every believer (vv.1)?

_____
_____
_____

6. *Who* does Paul state should be the focus of our prayers (vv. 1-2)?

_____
_____
_____

7. *Why* does Paul want Believers to pray in this regard (vv. 2-3)?

_____
_____
_____

8. *What* aspect of God's character serves as the basis for prayer in this regard (v. 4)?

_____
_____
_____

> **"There was a widow in that city,
> and she kept coming to him, saying,
> 'Give me legal protection from my opponent.'"
> Luke 18:3**

Throughout the Old Testament, over and over again, God linked widows and orphans to the need for justice (Exodus 22:22-24; Deuteronomy 10:18; Psalm 68:5; Isaiah 1:17). There were numerous widows throughout the text of Scripture who had been left in very difficult situations.

"Widows were often left with no means of support. If her husband left an estate, she did not inherit it, although provision for her upkeep would be made. If she remained in her husband's family, she had an inferior, almost servile, position. If she returned to her family, the money exchanged at the wedding had to be given back. Widows were so victimized that they were often sold as slaves for debt."[1]

---

[1] Klyne R. Snodgrass *Stories With Intent* ; Wm. B. Eerdmans Publishing Co., Grand Rapids/Cambridge. 453

Mysteries of the Kingdom Revealed

If a heartless, wretched man was the presiding judge over their case, you can understand how they could despair and lose heart.

9. Below are five widows who faced overwhelming hardship in their life. Although their story does not include begging and pleading for justice from an unjust judge, their situation was extremely difficult. Read each story below and describe the circumstances that could have caused each widow to lose heart.

    A.   **The Widow of Zarephath (I Kings 17:9-24)**

    _____
    _____
    _____
    _____

    B.   **Naomi (Ruth 1:1-5; 2:1-3; 4:13-17)**

    _____
    _____
    _____
    _____

    C.   **The Widow of Nain (Luke 7:11-15)**

    _____
    _____
    _____
    _____

    D.   **The Widow and her offering (Luke 21:1-4)**

    _____
    _____
    _____
    _____

    E.   **The Mourning Widows (Acts 9:39-41)**

    _____
    _____
    _____
    _____

The widow in the parable had been severely mistreated. "Give me legal protection from my opponent" she demanded. We are not told the nature of the problem or who the opponent was. Any number of things could have been the cause of the injustice she experienced, from her home being devoured to financial resources being swindled. She was in desperate need of a judge who would execute justice and equity according to God's law. She took up the matter with a judge, no doubt expecting justice but instead receiving disdain and rejection. Again and again the judge ignored her and would have nothing to do with her.

We know that the situation was urgent and dire because Jesus said "she kept coming to him." We can confidently say that the widow was in a horrifying trial of suffering. While the Parable of the Unjust Judge is not about trials, the fact that we as believers are going to face trials in life cannot be overlooked. Let's take another sidebar and consider how the Bible instructs believers to face trials in life.

10. Look up the following verses and jot down all that you learn about trials and how God uses them for His glory.

    A.   **Psalm 119:71**

    B.   **James 1:2-5**

    C.   **Romans 5:1-5**

    D.   **I Peter 4:12-13**

Mysteries of the Kingdom Revealed

    E.   **I Peter 5:8-10**

    _____
    _____
    _____
    _____

11.   How did Paul face his trial in **II Corinthians 12:7-10**? Jot down your thoughts and observations on the lines below.

_____
_____
_____
_____

When we do not understand that God uses the trials He allows in our life, they can become an easy tool of the enemy to bring about discouragement, feelings of defeat, and despair. They can be the cause of giving up on prayer and even giving up on God.

12.   How do the words of Jesus in **John 16:33** encourage and comfort you in your trials? Write your thoughts below.

_____
_____
_____
_____

Facing trials the way God intends will only occur as we faithfully pray and not lose heart in the midst of those trials.

> **"For a while he was unwilling; but afterward he said to himself,**
> **'Even though I do not fear God nor respect man,**
> **yet because this widow bothers me, I will give her legal protection,**
> **otherwise by continually coming she will wear me out.'"**
> **Luke 18:4-5**

The Greek word ὑπωπιζω *(hypopizo)*, translated "wear me out," means to strike in the face, a blow to the eye or to treat roughly.[4] Notice carefully the contrast between the two characters in the parable that Jesus masterfully taught.

---

[4] *Strong's Exhaustive Concordance of the Bible*, Nashville, TN: Abingdon Publishers, 1980, 75 (Greek Dictionary of the New Testament #5299).

A powerful yet ruthless and inhumane judge was overtaken by a helpless and destitute widow. How did this occur? Persistence!

Fear of God did not move the corrupt judge to act rightly towards the widow because he had no fear of God. Respect for people did not move the corrupt judge to act rightly towards the widow because he had no respect for people. <u>Persistence</u> caused the judge to respond rightly towards the widow. Perhaps the persistence of the widow created anxiety in the judge. Perhaps the persistence of the widow was *hypopizo* (a black eye) to the judge and therefore motivated him to "give her legal protection" (Luke 18:5).

> **"And the Lord said, 'Hear what the unrighteous judge said...'**
> **Now will not God bring about justice for His elect who cry to Him day and night,**
> **and will He delay long over them?**
> **I tell you that He will bring about justice for them quickly.**
> **However, when the Son of Man comes, will He find faith on the earth?"**
> **Luke 18:6-8**

13. Consider the stark contrast between the unjust Judge and God the Father. What do you think Jesus wanted the disciples to recognize about the character of His Father?

    _____
    _____
    _____
    _____

14. How does knowing this truth about God enable you to not lose heart in prayer?

    _____
    _____
    _____
    _____

15. How do you think "cry to Him day and night" relates to "will He find faith on the earth?"

    _____
    _____
    _____
    _____
    _____
    _____

Mysteries of the Kingdom Revealed

As we close our study, let's consider how we are to approach God when we cry out to Him. Think about your heart attitude when you go before God in prayer. In the chart below are eight principles of prayer. Meditate on each principle and answer each corresponding question in the box provided.

HOW ARE BELIEVERS TO APPROACH GOD WHEN WE "CRY OUT TO HIM?"		
We are to approach God	*Humbly* I Peter 5:6-7	What does it mean to humble yourself?
We are to approach God	*Submissively* I John 5:14-15	Why is aligning our will to God's will necessary?
We are to approach God	*Boldly* Hebrews 4:16	What does it mean to approach God boldly?
We are to approach God	*Dependently* Psalm 121:1-8	How is dependence on God manifested in prayer?
We are to approach God	*Expectantly* Hebrews 11:6	In what ways does God reward the believer?
We are to approach God	*Reverently* Hebrews 5:7	How do we show reverence to God in prayer?
We are to approach God	*Thankfully* Philippians 4:6	What does thankfulness demonstrate to God?

We are to approach God	*Persistently* Luke 18:1	How does growing weary hinder prayer?

**"By Your abundant lovingkindness
I will enter Your house,
At Your holy temple I will bow in reverence for You."
Psalm 5:7**

O SPIRIT OF GOD,

Help my infirmities;
When I am pressed down with a load of sorrow,
Perplexed and knowing not what to do,
Slandered and persecuted,
Made to feel the weight of the cross,
Help me, I pray thee.

If thou seest in me any wrong thing encouraged,
Any evil desire cherished, any delight that is not thy delight,
Any habit that grieves thee,
Any nest of sin in my heart, then grant me the kiss of thy forgiveness,
And teach my feet to walk the way of thy commandments.
Deliver me from carking care, and make me a happy, holy person;
Help me to walk the separated life with firm and brace step,
And to wrestle successfully against weakness;

Teach me to laud, adore, and magnify thee, with the music of heaven,
And make me a perfume of praiseful gratitude to thee.
I do not crouch at thy feet as a slave before a tyrant,
But exult before thee as a son with a father,
Give me power to live as thy child in all my actions,
And to exercise sonship by conquering self,
Preserve me from the intoxication that comes of prosperity;
Sober me when I am glad with a joy that comes not from thee.

Lead me safely on to the eternal kingdom,
Not asking whether the road be rough or smooth,
I request only to see the face of him I love,
To be content with bread to eat,
With raiment to put on,
If I can be brought to thy house in peace.

– The Valley of Vision
Page 103

PERSONAL REFLECTIONS

THE PRODIGAL SON

THE PRODIGAL SON

(Luke 15:11-32)

"And He said, "A man had two sons. The younger of them said to his father, 'Father, give me the share of the estate that falls to me.' So he divided his wealth between them. And not many days later, the younger son gathered everything together and went on a journey into a distant country, and there he squandered his estate with loose living. Now when he had spent everything, a severe famine occurred in that country, and he began to be impoverished. So he went and hired himself out to one of the citizens of that country, and he sent him into his fields to feed swine. And he would have gladly filled his stomach with the pods that the swine were eating, and no one was giving anything to him. But when he came to his senses, he said, 'How many of my father's hired men have more than enough bread, but I am dying here with hunger! I will get up and go to my father, and will say to him, 'Father, I have sinned against heaven, and in your sight; I am no longer worthy to be called your son; make me as one of your hired men.' So he got up and came to his father. But while he was still a long way off, his father saw him and felt compassion for him, and ran and embraced him and kissed him. And the son said to him, 'Father, I have sinned against heaven and in your sight; I am no longer worthy to be called your son.' But the father said to his slaves, 'Quickly bring out the best robe and put it on him, and put a ring on his hand and sandals on his feet; and bring the fattened calf, kill it, and let us eat and celebrate; for this son of mine was dead and has come to life again; he was lost and has been found.' And they began to celebrate."

"Now his older son was in the field, and when he came and approached the house, he heard music and dancing. And he summoned one of the servants and began inquiring what these things could be. And he said to him, 'Your brother has come, and your father has killed the fattened calf because he has received him back safe and sound.' But he became angry and was not willing to go in; and his father came out and began pleading with him. But he answered and said to his father, 'Look! For so many years I have been serving you and I have never neglected a command of yours; and yet you have never given me a young goat, so that I might celebrate with my friends; but when this son of yours came, who has devoured your wealth with prostitutes, you killed the fattened calf for him.' And he said to him, 'Son, you have always been with me, and all that is mine is yours. But we had to celebrate and rejoice, for this brother of yours was dead and has begun to live, and was lost and has been found.'"

THE PRODIGAL SON
Lost And Found

Theme: A father's longing for the return of his son

Scripture: Luke 15:11-32

Occasion: Jesus wanted to show that God welcomed into His kingdom those who society shunned and discarded.

Overview: The Parable of the Prodigal Son is the last of three parables that all speak of joy over the repentant sinner. In each consecutive parable, the focus is the joy that takes place. In the Parable of the Lost Sheep, the focus is joy in heaven (Luke 15:7). In the Parable of the Lost Coin, the focus is joy amongst the angels of God (Luke 15:10). In the Parable of the Prodigal Son, joy is manifested by the father. The father represents God who Himself rejoices over a repentant sinner (Luke 15:23, 32).

Heart Preparation: "For a day in your courts is better than a thousand outside. I would rather stand at the threshold of the house of my God than dwell in the tents of wickedness. For the Lord God is a sun and shield; the Lord gives grace and glory; no good thing does He withhold from those who walk uprightly" (Psalm 84:10-11).

THE PRODIGAL SON
Lost And Found

> "I will arise and go to Jesus
> He will embrace me in His arms,
> In the arms of my dear Savior,
> Oh there are ten thousand charms."
> – Joseph Hart

It is said that "there is joy in the presence of the angels of God over one sinner who repents" (Luke 15:10). When I think about The Parable of the Prodigal Son, it reminds me of the words of another favorite hymn of mine, "Come, Ye Sinners, Poor And Needy." The chorus of that hymn is written above. "I will arise and go to Jesus" is what every Christian parent of a prodigal wants to hear, there are no sweeter words to their ears. How much more so of our heavenly Father? How much more does He want to hear those words from the lips of sinners?

When he "came to his senses," the prodigal son said "I will get up and go to my father..." (Luke 15:17-18). Only God can awaken a sinner. Only God can give eyes that see and hearts that desire Him. Only God can cause a man or woman to arise and go to Jesus!

When I think about the parable I also think about the devastating decision the son made to leave home. I think about the deep heartache the father must have felt, no longer able to reason with his son, to warn his son about the snares of life or protect his son. I can imagine the father fighting back tears as he watched his son gather his belongings and walk out. Where would he go? What would he do for the rest of his life? Will I ever see him again? Will he follow through on what I have taught him? Was I thorough in preparing him to be a man? What did I neglect to teach him? Will he succeed on his own or will he fail? When life implodes on him will he have the sense to come home?

Perhaps these were some of the questions on the mind of the father as he watched his son leave. Perhaps he also thought about the words of Solomon that warn "...wealth certainly makes itself wings like an eagle that flies toward the heavens" (Proverbs 23:5).
While the father would hope to see his son again, he most likely knew he would never see the money he gave his son again.

Jesus had a masterful way of painting word pictures in the various parables He taught. The prodigal son is filled with a variety of snapshots that beautifully capture the way God the Father loves and responds to wayward children. Just as the father in the parable ran to his son at first glance, so our heavenly Father came after His elect even when we were in a far away country. By paving the way of salvation through Jesus Christ, Our Father provided for His elect to come.

1. How do the following verses give evidence to the fact that God provided for His elect?

   A. **Genesis 3:15**

   B. **Isaiah 53:10**

   C. **Romans 5:8**

   D. **II Corinthians 5:21**

As we begin our study of the prodigal son, keep in mind that the parable was taught in response to the Pharisees and Scribes who "began to grumble, saying, 'This man receives sinners and eats with them'" (Luke 15:2). Jesus wanted to teach the self-righteous Pharisees that He was not only concerned about but also loved society's outcast. He welcomed people who were discarded and considered unworthy of redemption by the religious leaders of His day. The three characters in the parable coincide with the nature of Jesus' audience. The prodigal son represented the tax gatherers and sinners. The older brother represented the Pharisees and religious leaders. The father represented God the Father.

Also keep in mind that while Jesus embraced and welcomed "sinners" into His kingdom, the Pharisees vigorously opposed them. Look up **Matthew 23:4, 13**.

2. How were the Pharisees working in direct opposition to Jesus and the kingdom of heaven?

_____
_____
_____
_____
_____

> **"A man had two sons.**
> **The younger of them said to his father,**
> **'Father, give me the share of the estate that falls to me.'**
> **So he divided his wealth between them.**
> **And not many days later, the younger son gathered everything together**
> **And went on a journey into a distant country,**
> **And there he squandered his estate with loose living."**
> **Luke 15:11-13**

3. How would you define the word prodigal?

_____
_____
_____
_____

Some parents can relate to the parable of the prodigal son because they have experienced it in some manner. Some parents were once prodigals themselves.

We are not told why the younger son wanted to leave his father's home but we certainly know what became of him after he left. We are not told why the father did not rebuke his son but instead complied and gave him his inheritance. It must have been shocking and insulting to the father to realize that his son cared more for what he could get from his father than for his father.

An inheritance was something received after the death of a parent yet the younger son had no shame in asking for his prematurely. It was the equivalent of saying "I wish you were dead."[1]

---

[1] Simon J. Kistemaker *The Parables*. Grand Rapids: Baker, 1980

Mysteries of the Kingdom Revealed

4. Although there was no mention of his mother in the story, what thoughts and concerns might be on the mind and heart of a mother dealing with a prodigal child?

_____
_____
_____
_____
_____
_____

5. What comfort does God offer to mothers who are experiencing the heartache and disappointment of a prodigal child?

_____
_____
_____
_____
_____
_____

**"And not many days later, the younger son gathered everything together
And went on a journey into a distant country,
And there he squandered his estate with loose living."
Luke 15:13**

It was clear that the young man had no intentions of returning home. There were no "goodbyes." There were no "thank you's." There was no "I love you, dad." There was no appreciation voiced or shown for the years of care and the lessons learned from a loving father. The inheritance was divided and the younger son took his share and left.

In the Jewish society, there were laws regarding how inheritances were typically divided. The oldest brother got a double share (Deuteronomy 21:17), while subsequent brothers got a single share.

When there were only two brothers, as in the parable, the older brother would get two thirds of the estate, and the younger brother would get one third.[2]

---

[2] Klyne R. Snodgrass *Stories With Intent*; Wm. B. Eerdmans Publishing Co., Grand Rapids/Cambridge. 126, 131

> **"Now when he had spent everything,
> a severe famine occurred in that country, and he began to be impoverished.
> So he went and hired himself out to one of the citizens of that country,
> And he sent him into his fields to feed swine.
> And he would have gladly filled his stomach
> with the pods that the swine were eating,
> And no one was giving anything to him. But when he came to his senses, he said,
> 'How many of my father's hired men have more than enough bread,
> But I am dying here with hunger! I will get up and go to my father,
> And will say to him, 'Father, I have sinned against heaven, and in your sight;
> I am no longer worthy to be called your son; make me as one of your hired men.'
> So he got up and came to his father. But while he was still a long way off,
> His father saw him and felt compassion for him,
> And ran and embraced him and kissed him."**
> **Luke 15:14-20**

The story began on a sad note. With the entire sum of his inheritance in tow, the youngest son set off for a "distant country" (Luke 15:13). His immaturity and inability to care for himself was evidenced in the fact that he "squandered his estate with loose living" (Luke 15:13). One bad decision after another and one wrong choice after another left him divested of all he once had. All that his father had worked so hard to acquire for his son's future was gone.

He fell on unimaginably hard times due to a famine and the fact that "no one was giving anything to him" (Luke 15:16). He ended up having to work for a citizen of the country who sent him "into his fields to feed swine" (Luke 15:15).

Sin will take you so utterly low and then abandon you. What happened to all the fun and good times the young man daydreamed about and planned for in the distant country? I can't imagine the thoughts that went through his mind every day he spent in the company of swine.

As a Jew, the prodigal would have been taught from childhood that pigs were cursed and ceremonially unclean animals and touching them or doing anything with them was in direct violation of God's law (Leviticus 11:7). So destitute and ruined was he that far from a curse, the pigs were a source through which he considered obtaining nourishment (Luke 15:16).

However, that disgusting thought was short lived and the story began to take a wonderful and dramatic turn when he "came to his senses" (Luke 15:17).

Mysteries of the Kingdom Revealed

6. What did the prodigal realize after coming to his senses (Luke 15:17)?

_____
_____
_____
_____

7. What do you learn about repentance from the prodigal's statement in Luke 15:18-19?

_____
_____
_____
_____

After a series of horribly wrong choices and circumstances that caused him to hit rock bottom, the prodigal finally made a wise choice, a choice that turned his whole life around. He chose to live. I'm not just talking about physical life but spiritual life, eternal life, the only life that matters. The prodigal son had a spiritual change of heart because God got involved.

8. According to **Ezekiel 11:19-20**, what does God do to every sinner with which He involves Himself? What is the corresponding result of that involvement?

_____
_____
_____
_____
_____

God got involved in the young man's life and the instant that took place, everything about him changed. He no longer desired to be in the distant country but instead to be home (Luke 15:17). He no longer desired to be separated from his father but "got up and came to his father" (Luke 15:20). He no longer felt entitled to take from his father but to serve his father (Luke 15:19). His attitude about life had changed. The pride that once ruled his heart was replaced with humility. His new heart was evidenced in the fact that he acknowledged his sin was first and foremost against God and also against his father (Luke 15:18). His new heart was evidenced in the fact that he repented and turned from a life of sin and debauchery and returned to his father (Luke 15:20).

I can not imagine the surge of excitement the father felt in his soul as he saw a figure in the far distance coming towards him. Perhaps he said to himself, "Could that be my son?" However, before he finished the question, he bolted into a full sprint towards the figure. It was very undignified and shameful for a man in that culture to run but it showed the father's deep love for his son and joy that he was alive and coming home.

9. What do you learn about forgiveness from the father's reaction at the very sight of his son (Luke 15:20)?

___

> **"And the son said to him,**
> **'Father, I have sinned against heaven and in your sight;**
> **I am no longer worthy to be called your son.'**
> **But the father said to his slaves,**
> **'Quickly bring out the best robe and put it on him,**
> **and put a ring on his hand and sandals on his feet;**
> **and bring the fattened calf, kill it, and let us eat and celebrate;**
> **for this son of mine was dead and has come to life again;**
> **he was lost and has been found.'"**
> **Luke 15:21-24a**

Just as he rehearsed, the prodigal began confessing his sin. Before he could finish saying what he had planned to say, his father interrupted and ordered "the best robe" be put on him, a ring on his hand and sandals for his feet.

10. How are the actions of the father a picture of the redemption of Christ?

___

> **"And they began to celebrate."**
> **Luke 15:24b**

Mysteries of the Kingdom Revealed

Sweet words for an incredibly beautiful ending. Everyone was in a festive, celebratory mood. Fun, laughter, and smiles filled the faces of the many guests who had gathered to rejoice over the return of the young man who had acted so foolishly that it nearly cost him his life. The story had certainly taken a dramatic turn from its sad and solemn beginning. It seemed to be headed in the direction of a "happily ever after" ending.

However, as life is true to form, there are no such things as "happily ever after" endings, at least not this side of heaven!

> **"Now his older son was in the field,**
> **And when he came and approached the house,**
> **He heard music and dancing. And he summoned one of the servants**
> **And began inquiring what these things could be.**
> **And he said to him, 'Your brother has come,**
> **And your father has killed the fattened calf**
> **Because he has received him back safe and sound.'"**
> **But he became angry and was not willing to go in;**
> **And his father came out and began pleading with him.**
> **But he answered and said to his father,**
> **'Look! For so many years I have been serving you**
> **And I have never neglected a command of yours;**
> **And yet you have never given me a young goat,**
> **So that I might celebrate with my friends;**
> **But when this son of yours came,**
> **Who has devoured your wealth with prostitutes,**
> **You killed the fattened calf for him.'"**
> **Luke 15:25-30**

11. What thoughts come to mind after reading the verses above?

_____
_____
_____
_____

Almost immediately as the older son came on the scene, the story plummeted and took an unexpected turn in the most outrageous manner. The title of the parable could easily be, The Parable of the Prodigal "Sons." There were two prodigals, one who left and one who remained. The younger traveled to a "distant country," the older, although physically near, was distant in his heart, with an appearance of obedience and righteousness.

Notice again what he said to his father during his angry tirade in **Luke 15:29-30**.

The older brother viewed himself as:

– the loyal son	"For so many years I have been serving you..." (v. 29)
– the "good" son	"I have never neglected a command of yours..." (v. 29)
– the underappreciated son	"You have never given me a young goat so I could celebrate with my friends..." (v. 29)
– the worthy son	"But when this son of yours came..." (v. 30)

Remember, the older brother represented the Pharisees and religious leaders in the crowd listening to Jesus teach. As I thought about the older brother's assessment of himself, it reminded me of another parable in which a Pharisee talked about himself to God.

Read **Luke 18:9-14**.

12. What reason did Jesus give for teaching the parable?

13. Based on the Pharisee's prayer, how did he view attaining righteousness?

14. According to **II Corinthians 5:21**, how is righteousness granted?

15. Based on **Luke 18:9**, what is a manifestation of trusting in oneself as righteous?

Mysteries of the Kingdom Revealed

God said, "Man looks at the outward appearance, but the Lord looks at the heart" (I Samuel 16:7). The Pharisee in Luke 9 raised his self-righteous banner to God on the basis of outward behavior. And what a banner: "I fast twice a week; I pay tithes of all I get" he proclaimed in his prayer (Luke 18:12).

The Pharisees of Jesus' day kept the letter of the Old Testament law meticulously and strategically. On the basis of merit alone, they thought they were outstanding and deserving of the highest recognition. However, notice what Jesus thought of the Pharisees. Read **Matthew 23:25-28**.

16. How does Matthew 23:28 apply to the older brother in the parable?
    _____
    _____
    _____

17. According to **Matthew 23:11-12**, what did Jesus want the disciples as well as you and me to understand and put into practice?
    _____
    _____
    _____

The Pharisee fully expected an applause from God, just as the older brother in the parable expected recognition from his father. The singing, dancing, and celebrating of a pleasure-seeking rebel was too much to take. Rebels shouldn't get parties they should get punished, that is the conclusion of the self-righteous. Once the older brother opened his mouth, his hateful character was exposed.

Jesus said, "The things that proceed out of the mouth come from the heart, and those defile the man. For out of the heart come evil thoughts, murders, adulteries, fornications, thefts, false witness, slanders" (Matthew 15:19).

On the surface the older brother's response may seem reasonable. However, consider again what transpired in the story.

FACT #1

He heard music and dancing. He summoned a servant. He inquired about the party. (Luke 15:25-27)	Why waste time calling a servant over to explain the reason for the party? Why not go in and see for yourself? Surely he knew his father well enough to know that he would not throw a party for no good reason.

The Prodigal Son

Your Thoughts:

_____
_____
_____
_____
_____

FACT #2

He became angry. (Luke 15:28)	A clear sign that his younger brother's return was not good news. He had no relationship with his brother. He was "in the field" (Luke 15:25) when his brother returned and was probably there when his brother initially left.

Your Thoughts:

_____
_____
_____
_____
_____

FACT #3

He refused to enter in to the celebration. (Luke 15:28)	The older brother chose not to speak to his father until his father spoke to him first. The father "came out and began imploring him" (Luke 15:28).

Your Thoughts:

_____
_____
_____
_____
_____

FACT #4

He spoke disrespectfully to his father.	"Look for so many years I have been serving you" (Luke 15:29). What do you think of that statement? How do you think the older son viewed his relationship with his father?

Your Thoughts:

_____
_____
_____
_____
_____

The statement of the older brother indicated that his relationship with his father was skewed. It is obvious they did not have a normal father/son relationship. He said, "For so many years I have been serving, you..." The Greek word δουλεύω (*douleuo*) translated "serving" means to enslave, to serve as a slave.[3] Perhaps the older brother saw himself as nothing more than a slave to his father.

His attitude and disposition towards his father was brought on by the enemy. This is what the enemy does. He lies. He distorts. He alters the thoughts of an individual and leads them to think negatively about others, even the people closest to them.

It happened in the Garden of Eden with his first victim, Eve. "You surely shall not die," Satan told her. "For God knows that in the day you eat from it your eyes will be opened and you will be like God, knowing good and evil" (Genesis 3:4-5). That statement set the stage for Eve's own desires to become front and center. It opened her mind to an alternative way of living. A way of living that excluded regard for the Word of God. A way of living that suggested God had a character flaw and therefore should not be trusted. A way of living that gave rise to thoughts of entitlement and "personal rights." Once Satan succeeded in misleading Eve in how she thought about God and His Word, autonomy and self-fulfillment became the goal. Eve acted according to what made her feel good about herself and her future. Eve acted according to what was practical and what made sense in her skewed thinking.

Who knows what Satan lied about to the older brother. His next statement to his father was further evidence of faulty thinking (Luke 15:29). The older brother said "I have never neglected a command of yours." Really? Did he really believe that he had <u>never</u> neglected his father's commands? That statement can only be said of one Man, the GodMan, Jesus Christ. He never neglected one of His Father's commands (John 14:31).

The older brother had an abnormal relationship with his father partly because he viewed his father as a task master rather than the loving, caring, generous father that he was.

---

[3]Verlyn D. Verbrugge *The NIV Theological Dictionary of New Testament Words,* (Zondervan Publishing House, Grand Rapids MI, 2000), 348.

The Prodigal Son

Unfortunately, people today have a distorted view of God the Father and even more so of Jesus Christ and Christianity.

18. What are some common excuses people give for rejecting Jesus Christ and Christianity?

19. People are blinded by Satan from the truth and have chosen to believe his lies. Read **I John 5:3** and write what it says about God on the lines below.

20. Read **Matthew 11:28**. What does Jesus offer to anyone who will listen and why?

FACT #5

| He accused his father of playing favorites. (Luke 15:29) | The older brother was a self-righteous hypocrite. He indicated that he related to his father on a slave to master level. What slave expects his master to throw a party for him from time to time? |

Your Thoughts:

Mysteries of the Kingdom Revealed

FACT #6

| He was bitterly resentful towards his father. (Luke 15:30) | The commands of the father that the older brother neglected were racking up. No love. No compassion. No forgiveness. No respect. No gratitude for his brother's safe return, just to name a few. |

Your Thoughts:

_____
_____
_____
_____
_____

FACT #7

| He demonstrated wholesale disregard and hatred for his brother (Luke 15:30). | The older brother could not bring himself to say "my brother." Instead, "this son of yours" was how he referred to him. He had no problem verbally attacking his father and slandering his brother. |

Your Thoughts:

_____
_____
_____
_____
_____

FACT #8

| He was treated with love, patience and respect by his father (Luke 15:31). | The father immediately left the celebration when his older son refused to participate. The father wanted his older son with him and went to great lengths, appealing to him and acknowledging his loyalty. |

Your Thoughts:

_____
_____
_____
_____
_____

As stated earlier, there were two prodigal sons, one came to his senses and returned to his loving father. He brought nothing with him. He had absolutely nothing to offer his father. He accepted the overwhelming kindness and generosity of his father. Although his sin perhaps was known by all, he humbly entered into joy and fellowship with family and friends.

However, regarding the other son, we are left wondering what happened. How did he respond to his father's passionate appeal? Did he repent and let go of his anger and animosity? Did he enter the celebration and approach his brother with forgiveness and genuine love? Or did he remain outside in his own self-righteous world?

Self-righteousness along with self-deception are probably two of the most often used tools of Satan to blind people from the truth about themselves. Excusing, comparing, justifying and overlooking their own sin, while at the same time accusing others, refusing to forgive others and magnifying the sin of others, all stem from a self-righteous attitude. It is what the Bible condemns again and again (Romans 10:3, I John 1:8,10).

There were those in Jesus' day "who trusted in themselves that they were righteous" (Luke 18:9) and there are such people in our day as well. If you are trusting in anything other than the shed blood of the Lord Jesus Christ to be in right standing with God, you are no different than the Pharisees whom Jesus opposed and vigorously spoke out against.

In closing, I want you to meditate on the words of a familiar hymn.

"My hope is built on nothing less than Jesus' blood and righteousness;
I dare not trust the sweetest frame,
But wholly lean on Jesus' name.
When He shall come with trumpet sound,
Oh, may I then in Him be found;
Dressed in His righteousness alone,
Faultless to stand before the throne.
On Christ the solid rock I stand, all other ground is sinking sand."
– Edward Mote

O SAVIOUR OF SINNERS,

Thy name is excellent,
Thy glory high,
Thy compassions unfailing,
Thy condescension wonderful,
Thy mercy tender.
I bless thee for the discoveries, invitations, promises of the gospel,
For in them is pardon for rebels,
Liberty for captives,
Health for the sick,
Salvation for the lost.
I come to thee in thy beloved name of Jesus;
Re-impress thy image upon my soul;
Raise me above the smiles and frowns of the world,
Regarding it as a light thing to be judged by men;
May thy approbation be my only aim,
Thy Word my one rule.
Make me to abhor that which grieves thy Holy Spirit,
To suspect consolations of a worldly nature,
To shun a careless way of life,
To reprove evil,
To instruct with meekness those who oppose me,
To be gentle and patient towards all men,
To be not only a professor but an example of the gospel,
Displaying in every relation, office, and condition
Its excellency, loveliness and advantages.
How little have I illustrated my principles
And improved my privileges!
How seldom have I served my generation!
How often have I injured and not recommended my redeemer!
How few are those blessed through me!
In many things I have offended,
In all come short of thy glory;
Pardon my iniquity, for it is great.

– The Valley of Vision
Page 58

PERSONAL REFLECTIONS

THE PURSUIT OF LIFE

THE PURSUIT OF LIFE:
THE NARROW GATE vs. THE WIDE GATE

(Matthew 7:13-27)

"Enter through the narrow gate; for the gate is wide and the way is broad that leads to destruction and many are those who enter through it. For the gate is small and the way is narrow that leads to life and there are few who find it. Beware of the false prophets, who come to you in sheep's clothing, but inwardly are ravenous wolves. You will know them by their fruits. Grapes are not gathered from thorn bushes nor figs from thistles are they? So every good tree bears good fruit, but the bad tree bears bad fruit. A good tree cannot produce bad fruit, nor can a bad tree produce good fruit. Every tree that does not bear good fruit is cut down and thrown into the fire. So then you will know them by their fruits.

Not everyone who says to Me, Lord, Lord, will enter the kingdom of heaven, but he who does the will of My Father who is in heaven will enter. Many will say to Me on that day, Lord, Lord, did we not prophesy in Your name, and in Your name cast out demons, and in Your name perform many miracles? And then I will declare to them, I never knew you; depart from Me, you who practice lawlessness.

Therefore everyone who hears these words of Mine and acts on them, may be compared to a wise man who built his house on the rock. And the rain fell, and the floods came, and the winds blew and slammed against that house; and yet it did not fall for it had been founded on the rock. Everyone who hears these words of Mine and does not act on them, will be like a foolish man who built his house on the sand. The rain fell and the floods came, and the winds blew and slammed against that house; and it fell and great was its fall."

THE PURSUIT OF LIFE
Are You Among The Few Or The Many?

Theme: The Narrow Gate vs. The Wide Gate

Scripture: Matthew 7:13-27

Occasion: In light of the massive response of the people to His healing ministry, Jesus taught the Sermon On The Mount and the true way to eternal life.

Overview: There are two ways to travel; one is true and the other is false. One leads to eternal life and the other leads to eternal destruction. Jesus explains the two different roads in what we call "The Sermon On The Mount." He concluded His sermon with, "everyone who hears these words of Mine and acts on them, may be compared to a wise man who built his house on the rock" (Matthew 7:24).

Heart Preparation: "How blessed is the man who does not walk in the counsel of the wicked, nor stand in the path of sinners, nor sit in the seat of scoffers! But his delight is in the law of the Lord, and in His law he meditates day and night. He will be like a tree firmly planted by streams of water, which yields its fruit in its season and its leaf does not wither; and in whatever he does, he prospers." (Psalm 1:1-3)

THE PURSUIT OF LIFE:
THE NARROW GATE vs. THE WIDE GATE
Are You Among The Few Or The Many?

> **"There is a way which seems right to a man,
> But its end is the way of death."
> Proverbs 16:25**

Choices! What would life be without choices. You have had to make choices your entire life. In fact, everyday of your life is a day filled with choices. Some choices are repetitive such as, what time you will wake up in the morning, what you will wear and what you will eat for breakfast. Other choices require an investment of your time, your talent, or your resources. Some choices result in temporary consequences while others result in eternal consequences.

Adam and Eve were given a command by God but they chose to act upon what seemed right in their own eyes. As a result, mankind was plunged into the depths of destruction. They made a choice that resulted in eternal consequences.

In the Old Testament, Moses said to the Children of Israel,

> **"I call heaven and earth to witness against you today,
> That I have set before you life and death, the blessing and the curse.
> So choose life in order that you may live, you and your descendants."
> Deuteronomy 30:19**

Joshua continued the same theme when he uttered the following words,

> **"If it is disagreeable in your sight to serve the Lord,
> Choose for yourselves today whom you will serve...
> but as for me and my house, we will serve the Lord."
> Joshua 24:15**

Jeremiah was commanded to reiterate the words of Moses when he said,

Mysteries of the Kingdom Revealed

"Thus says the Lord, 'behold, I set before you the way of life and the way of death.'"
Jeremiah 21:8

In each one of those commands, a choice had to be made resulting in consequences that impacted one's life. At the conclusion of the Sermon on the Mount, the disciples and the crowd of followers heard a command and had a choice to make, also related to life. Jesus said,

"Enter through the narrow gate;
For the gate is wide and the way is broad that leads to destruction,
And many are those who enter through it.
For the gate is small and the way is narrow that leads to life,
And there are few who find it."
Matthew 7:13-14

1. Jesus mentioned two gates in the verses above. Contrast the two gates in the chart below, making a list of the differences and similarities.

GATE #1	GATE #2

2. Let's talk about life. According to the following verses, how is "earthly" life described?

   A. **James 4:14**
   _____

   B. **Psalm 144:4**
   _____

   C. **Psalm 90:12**
   _____

The Pursuit of Life

D. **Psalm 39:5**

E. **Isaiah 40:6-7**

F. **Hebrews 9:27**

3. According to the following verses, how is "eternal" life described?

   A. **John 1:4**

   B. **John 3:16**

   C. **John 5:24**

   D. **John 10:10**

   E. **John 10:28**

   F. **John 11:25**

   G. **John 14:6**

189

Mysteries of the Kingdom Revealed

4. What do the verses above teach you about the life Jesus came to offer?

_____
_____
_____
_____
_____

In the Sermon on the Mount, Jesus taught on what real kingdom life consist of and contrasted it with the fake and phony life of the Pharisees. Early on in the Sermon on the Mount, the reader is confronted with two very different ways of living.

After exhorting His listeners of the heart attitudes that should mark every believer's life, Jesus made a surprising statement.

5. Look up **Matthew 5:20** and write it on the lines below.

_____
_____
_____
_____
_____
_____

It would have been a virtual certainty that Jesus' statement sent shock waves through the crowds of people and the disciples. Of all the people who were expected to be heaven bound, the Pharisees and those who considered themselves religious would certainly be among the first. The notion that their righteousness was not held in high regard by Jesus was mind blowing.

Although the Bible declares that God loves righteousness (Psalm 33:5), there was something utterly reprehensible about the "righteousness" of the Pharisees. They looked good externally but their hearts were "full of hypocrisy and lawlessness" (Matthew 23:28). They were devoid of humility, compassion and love. They offered no repentance for their sin. They exercised no faith in Jesus Christ, in fact often times, they "picked up stones to throw at him" (John 8:59). And they gave no obedience to the law of God. These acts alone placed them squarely on the wide road headed for destruction.

Sadly, there are churches today filled with people just like the Pharisees. They don't see themselves as pharisaical and would condemn the actions and teachings of the Pharisees. However, ironically, these very same people are "trying to make heaven their home." They firmly believe and preach that "if you take one step, God will take two." They live according to the mantra, "If you do your best, God will do the rest." Rather than full obedience and submission to the Word of God, they devise their own methods and ways to spirituality by what seems right in their own eyes.

Anyone who seeks to be justified by religion or man-made spirituality is squarely on the wide road leading to destruction. Christ' righteousness however is marked by repentance, faith and obedience. Notice what He said about each one in the chart below.

Repentance	"Repent, for the kingdom of heaven is at hand" (Matthew 4:17).
Faith	"The time is fulfilled, and the kingdom of God is at hand; repent and believe in the gospel" (Mark 1:15).
Obedience	"Not everyone who says to Me, Lord, Lord will enter the kingdom of heaven, but he who does the will of My Father who is in heaven will enter" (Matthew 7:21).

When Jesus said, "enter through the narrow gate," it was repentance, faith and obedience to which He was referring. Repentance and faith provide entrance through the narrow gate, and obedience is a part of the narrow road that leads to life. You will not and can not have eternal life without them. Let's look at each of these a little closer.

"Repent for the kingdom of heaven is at hand" (Matthew 4:17), was the warning Jesus stated throughout His earthly ministry. Jesus spoke more often about heaven and hell than anything else. He urged all who would hear Him to "repent."

Read **Luke 13:1-5**.

Death does not discriminate! Whether you have royal blood running through your veins, have lived on public assistance your entire life, or anywhere in between, death is the common denominator for everyone. Danger and sudden death are lurking all around us, all the time. No one is immune to tragedies and calamities. Just recently the world watched yet another tragic scene of young kids and teens ambushed at a concert event in London, England. An arena filled with ordinary people, smiling, laughing, enjoying their day, enjoying the concert and no doubt looking forward to the next day, of which some would never see. Their lives were tragically and horrifically snuffed out by a terrorist attack.

A tragic event was the subject of discussion brought to the attention of Jesus in Luke 13.

Several Galileans were fatally wounded while in the process of offering a sacrifice to the Lord. A senseless killing of ordinary people who perhaps never thought that entering the temple that day would result in entering eternity.

6. How did Jesus respond to the report and what did He urge the crowd to do?

_____
_____
_____

When tragic events happen our natural tendency is to ask two questions, why did it happen and where was God? We may even begin to think that God causes tragedies. We think God gets so displeased with sinful people that sometimes He retaliates by causing tragic events to occur. When 9/11 took place there were people thinking along those same lines. Some people foolishly believed that God caused the attack because of the sinfulness of America.

Jesus responded to similar thinking when tragedy struck a group of Galileans. It wasn't that Jesus was being aloof or uncaring about the tragedy rather, He wanted the people to realize that the Galileans who lost their life in the temple, were no more righteous or unrighteous than they were. He wanted their focus to be on repentance and pursuing a life of obedience to His Word.

Life is fragile and life is temporary. The Psalmist made it clear when he said, "man is like a mere breath, his days are like a passing shadow" (Psalm 144:4). James said,

> "...you are just a vapor that appears for a little while
> and then vanishes away."
> James 4:14

The author of Hebrews said,

> "It is appointed for men to die once and after this comes judgment."
> Hebrews 9:27

Jesus wanted the people to consider their own life in light of eternity. He wanted them to understand that being in a right relationship with God was the only recourse they had against sudden death. A right relationship with God begins with repentance.

7. How do you define repentance?

8. What do you learn about repentance from the following verses? Write your thoughts on the lines below.

   A. **Acts 2:38**

   B. **Acts 3:19**

   C. **Acts 11:17-18**

   D. **Acts 17:30-31**

   E. **Acts 20:20-21**

   F. **Acts 26:19-20**

Mysteries of the Kingdom Revealed

The word "repentance" carries the idea of changing one's mind about sin and the consequences of that change of mind, which is turning completely from sinful living. It is a change of one's mind resulting in a change of one's actions. The Greek word μετ νοια *(metanoia)* translated repentance means to change one's mind, repent, be converted.[1] Repentance begins in the heart through the work of the Holy Spirit, causing you to sorrow over sin. In humility of heart, you recognize your utter wretchedness before a holy God. You then turn away from your sin and turn to God through exercising faith (trusting) in Him alone for forgiveness of your sin.

Obedience to the will and Word of God is the outgrowth of repentance and faith. You know you have genuinely repented and have genuine faith because you desire and strive to please the Lord. Let's continue, please read **Luke 13:6-9**

Jesus began to teach another parable about a fruitless fig tree. This short yet powerful parable reminds us of the graciousness and patience of the Lord. It also reiterates Jesus' warning to repent.

The man who owned the fig tree had patiently watched and waited for it to bear fruit but to no avail. Even after the passing of three years, still no fruit appeared. The obvious next step would have been to cut the tree down and perhaps start over with another tree. However, the keeper of the vineyard suggested to the owner that he should wait for a period of one more year for fruit to be born on the tree. If still no fruit after a year, the tree was to be cut down.

The parable teaches that one of the prime indicators of the existence of life in those who profess Christ, is fruitfulness. Bearing fruit in one's life is one of the most critical components of salvation. It is also evidence that you are traveling on the narrow road that leads to life. Jesus said,

> **"Every branch in Me that does not bear fruit,**
> **He takes away; and every branch that bears fruit,**
> **He prunes it so that it may bear more fruit.**
>
> **If anyone does not abide in Me,**
> **he is thrown away as a branch and dries up;**
> **and they gather them,**
> **and cast them into the fire and they are burned."**
> **John 15:2, 6**

---

[1] Verlyn D. Verbrugge, *The NIV Theological Dictionary of New Testament Words*, (Zondervan Publishing House, Grand Rapids MI, 2000), 819.

We have talked about repentance and faith that provides entrance into the narrow gate, however another aspect of repentance occurs while traveling on the narrow road. In desiring and striving to please the Lord, you are made more and more aware of your sin and need for on-going repentance. Listen to what Jesus told the disciples as He prepared to wash their feet in the upper room,

> **"Jesus said to him, 'He who has bathed needs only to wash his feet,
> but is completely clean; and you are clean, but not all of you.'
> For He knew the one who was betraying Him;
> for this reason He said, 'Not all of you are clean.'"**
> **John 13:10**

When Jesus said, "you are already clean," it meant the disciples had repented of their sins and had entered through the narrow gate. When Jesus said, "he who has bathed needs only to wash his feet, but is completely clean," it meant receiving forgiveness and cleansing that comes through <u>daily</u> repentance of sins committed. We sin every day, multiple times a day and we are to repent of those sins each time. As stated earlier, repentance is ongoing throughout the journey leading to life.

Notice the opening sentences of David's penitent prayer in Psalm 51.

> **"Be gracious to me, O God, according to Your lovingkindness;
> According to the greatness of Your compassion blot out my transgressions.
> Wash me thoroughly from my iniquity and cleanse me from my sin.
> For I know my transgressions, and my sin is ever before me.
> Against You, You only, I have sinned and done what is evil in Your sight,
> So that You are justified when You speak and blameless when You judge."**
> **Psalm 51:1-4**

David used three different words in his confession to describe his wrong doing. He used the words "transgression," "iniquity," and "sin." All three words have the same basic meaning of lawlessness before God. However, you will notice from the chart below that each one carries a slightly different nuance of meaning.

"Cleanse me from my **sin**" "My **sin** is ever before me" "Against You, You only, I have **sinned**..."	*Sin* means to miss the mark. It can refer to doing something against God or against a person. Sin is the general term for disobedience to the law of God.
"Wash me thoroughly from my **iniquity**..."	*Iniquity* means pre-meditated choice. David thought through and planned out the killing of Bathsheba's husband Uriah. Iniquity also means a continuing on without repentance. David carried on with his life for an entire year before his confession to the Lord.
"Blot out my **transgressions**" "For I know my **transgressions** and my sin is ever before me."	*Transgression* refers to presumptuous sin. It means to choose to act, to intentionally disobey. It is wilful trespassing.[2] David after seeing Bathsheba bathing, sent and inquired about her and ordered messengers to bring her to him. "When she came to him, he lay with her" (II Samuel 11:4).

9. What does David's prayer of confession in Psalm 51:1-4 teach you about God? Write your thoughts below.

_____
_____
_____
_____
_____
_____

Repentance, faith, and obedience provide entrance through the narrow gate and repentance, faith, and obedience carry you along the narrow road that leads to life. We must continue trusting and believing in Christ(faith), we must continue confessing our sin and turning to Christ (repentance) and we must continue walking in the ways of Christ (obedience). These are the tenets of the Christian faith. These are the absolutes in the pursuit of life.

However, there is another gate. Jesus said,

---

[2]https://www.gotquestions.org/*repentance*.html

> **"...for the gate is wide
> and the way is broad that leads to destruction
> and many are those who enter through it."
> Matthew 7:13**

Scores of people are flocking to the wide gate. No one is prevented from entering nor turned away due to overcrowding. It would seem the more travelers who enter, the more room is made available for them. Apparently the gate is easy to find and easy to access. The problem is that the people traveling the wide road believe they will arrive at an endpoint called life only to discover that destruction awaits them. Jesus said,

> **"...Unless your righteousness surpasses that of the scribes and Pharisees,
> you will not enter the kingdom of heaven."
> Matthew 5:20**

After the above statement was made, Jesus began contrasting the righteousness of God with the false righteousness of the Pharisees. He began dismantling the self elevating, works oriented way of living that the scribes and Pharisees had established and vigorously promoted.

Matthew 5 contains the first six examples that Jesus used to demonstrate the faulty beliefs of the Pharisees. Matthew 6 contains the sinful actions that resulted from the faulty beliefs of the Pharisees.

10. In the charts below, explain the difference between the righteousness of the Pharisees and the righteousness of God.

MATTHEW 5:21-22

"You have heard...	"But I say to you...
that the ancients were told, you shall not commit murder and 'whoever commits murder shall be liable to the court.'"	that everyone who is angry with his brother shall be guilty before the court and whoever says to his brother, 'you good for nothing' shall be guilty before the supreme court; and whoever says, 'you fool,' shall be guilty enough to go into the fiery hell."

Mysteries of the Kingdom Revealed

What is the difference between the two statements?

MATTHEW 5:27-28

"You have heard...	"But I say to you...
that it was said, 'you shall not commit adultery.'"	that everyone who looks at a woman with lust for her has already committed adultery with her in his heart."

What is the difference between the two statements?

MATTHEW 5:31-32

"It was said...	"But I say to you...
'whoever sends his wife away, let him give her a certificate of divorce'	that everyone who divorces his wife, except for the reason of unchastity, makes her commit adultery; and whoever marries a divorced woman commits adultery."

What is the difference between the two statements?

MATTHEW 5:33-34

"Again, you have heard... that the ancients were told, 'you shall not make false vows, but shall fulfill your vows to the Lord.'"	"But I say to you... make no oath at all, either by heaven, for it is the throne of God, or by the earth, for it is the footstool of His feet, or by Jerusalem, for it is the city of the great King. Nor shall you make an oath by your head, for you cannot make one hair white or black. But let your statement be, 'yes, yes' or 'no, no; anything beyond these is of evil."
What is the difference between the two statements?	

MATTHEW 5:38-39

"You have heard... that it was said, 'an eye for an eye, and a tooth for a tooth.'"	"But I say to you... do not resist an evil person; but whoever slaps you on your right cheek, turn the other to him also."
What is the difference between the two statements?	

MATTHEW 5:43-44

"You have heard... that it was said, 'you shall love your neighbor and hate your enemy.'"	"But I say to you... love your enemies and pray for those who persecute you."
What is the difference between the two statements?	

11. Read **Matthew 6:1-4**. What was wrong with the way the Pharisees gave their offering? How do you see similar actions manifested today?

12. Read **Matthew 6:5-15**. What was wrong with the way the Pharisees offered their prayers? How do you see similar actions manifested today?

13. Read **Matthew 6:16-18**. What was wrong with the way the Pharisees practiced fasting? How do you see similar actions manifested today?

Jesus laid out a clear and concise argument against the rituals and practices of the scribes and Pharisees. Why did He do that? The Pharisees were attributing to God as though sanctioned by Him what was in reality man made religion. People naturally believe "if I am religious, I am righteous." "If I do enough good deeds, they will cancel out all of my bad deeds."

There were people in Jesus' day like the Pharisees who were religious but lost just as there are people in our day who are religious but lost. They have rejected Christ's way of righteousness and devised their own way which makes them appear righteous. They enter through the wide gate and travel comfortably on the wide road. It doesn't take much to be a religious person.

There are people who believe they are saved but are actually on the wide road. This is the point Jesus was making when He told an individual to "strive to enter through the narrow door; for many, I tell you, will seek to enter and will not be able" (Luke 13:24).

The wide road ultimately does not require you to change. You can simply add Jesus to your life and carry on with your life the way that best pleases you. The wide road does not require you to "love your enemies." It makes no sense to love people who are your enemies. The wide road does not require you to pray for those who persecute you. It makes no sense to pray for the very people who hurt and mistreat you. If you are offended by the church or experience a broken relationship in your church, you simply pack up and move on. You do not seek to be reconciled and you certainly do not forgive. If you become tired of and "fall out of love" with your spouse, you simply get out of the marriage. It's too hard and besides, you and your husband have "grown apart."
You are like the woman in Proverbs who "leaves the companion of her youth and forgets the covenant of her God" (Proverbs 2:17).

The wide road allows you to do what makes sense and seems right in the moment. The wide road is very accommodating and bends to your wishes and desires, allowing you to be you. However, the problem with you being you, is that you will not become like Christ and Christ will not be "formed in you" (Galatians 4:19). Sadly, you will one day hear Jesus say, "I never knew you; depart from Me, you who practice lawlessness" (Matthew 7:23).

However, I want you to notice one final comparison Jesus made in His sermon.

> **"Therefore everyone who hears these words of Mine and acts on them, may be compared to a wise man who built his house on the rock. And the rain fell, and the floods came,**

> **and the winds blew and slammed against that house;**
> **and yet it did not fall, for it had green founded on the rock.**
> **Everyone who hears these words of Mine and does not act on them,**
> **will be like a foolish man who built his house on the sand.**
> **The rain fell and the floods came,**
> **and the winds blew and slammed against that house;**
> **and it fell and great was its fall."**
> **Matthew 7:24-27**

We began our study of the parables of Jesus examining what it means to have "ears to hear" and as we close, our attention is once again focused on hearing. Jesus said only a foolish person would build a house on a foundation of sand. So it is that only a foolish person would listen to the warnings of Jesus and make no changes to align themselves to the truth of His Word.

What about you? Have you entered through the narrow gate? Are you on the narrow road that leads to life? It's not too late for you to enter.

Peter said,

> **"Therefore brethren, be all the more diligent**
> **To make certain about His calling and choosing you;**
> **For as long as you practice these things,**
> **You will never stumble."**
> **II Peter 1:10**

Paul said,

> **"Test yourselves to see if you are in the faith;**
> **Examine yourselves!**
> **Or do you not recognize that about yourselves,**
> **That Jesus Christ is in you- unless indeed you fail the test?"**
> **II Corinthians 13:5**

Jesus said,

> **"If anyone wishes to come after Me, he must deny himself,**
> **and take up his cross and follow Me.**
> **For whoever wishes to save his life will lose it;**
> **but whoever loses his life for My sake will find it."**

Matthew 16:24-25

Jesus also said,

**"Come to Me, all who are weary and heavy-laden,
and I will give you rest.
Take My yoke upon you and learn from me,
for I am gentle and humble in heart,
and you will find rest for your souls.
For My yoke is easy and My burden is light."
Matthew 11:28-30**

If you are not absolutely, unequivocally sure about your relationship with the Lord, you need to take Jesus up on His offer. He is offering Himself to you right now. He is offering eternal life to you right now. He is inviting you to enter through the narrow gate. The only way to eternal life is through Jesus Christ. You may be asking why must I go through Jesus Christ to have eternal life? Jesus said, "I am the way, the truth and the life, no one comes to the Father but through Me" (John 14:6).

God is holy and you are unholy and eternally ruined by sin. Sin is what separates you from God (Isaiah 59:2). Sin was punished in Christ Jesus and therefore He is the only way you have access to God the Father and to eternal life.

Jesus took the punishment that you should have experienced and by His shed blood on your behalf, satisfied the wrath of God (Isaiah 53:10). Because of what Jesus did, God chooses not to hold your sin against you but "as far as the east is from the west, so far has He removed your transgressions from you" (Psalm 103:12, emphasis added). All you have to do is receive the free gift of the Lord Jesus Christ. You can bow in prayer right where you are and receive Christ.

Paul said,

**"If you confess with your mouth that Jesus is Lord
and believe in your heart that God raised Him from the dead,
you will be saved."
(Romans 10:9)**

Jesus said,

**"Truly, truly, I say to you,
whoever hears My word and believes Him who sent Me has eternal life.**

He does not come into judgment, but has passed from death to life" (John 5:24).

It is my sincere prayer that you know the Lord Jesus Christ personally and commit to living a life that glorifies Him. It is my prayer that this Bible study has been a blessing to you. It is my prayer that this Bible study has deeply enriched your life and created an even greater hunger and thirst for godly righteousness. It was truly a labor of love that God brought about by His power and according to His will.

TO THE PRAISE AND GLORY OF HIS GREAT NAME!

GOD OF MY END,

It is my greatest, noblest pleasure
to be acquainted with Thee
and with my rational, immortal soul;
It is sweet and entertaining
to look into my being
when all my powers and passions
are united and engaged in pursuit of Thee,
when my soul longs and passionately breathes
after conformity to Thee and the full enjoyment of Thee;

No hours pass away with so much pleasure
as those spent in communion with Thee and with my heart.

O how desirable, how profitable to the Christian life
is a spirit of holy watchfulness
and godly jealousy over myself
when my soul is afraid of nothing
except grieving and offending Thee, the blessed God,
my Father and friend,
whom I then love and long to please,
rather than be happy in myself!

Knowing, as I do, that this is the pious temper,
worthy of the highest ambition,
and closest pursuit of intelligent creatures and holy Christians,
may my joy derive from glorifying and delighting Thee.
I long to fill all my time for Thee,
whether at home or in the way;
to place all my concerns in Thy hands;
to be entirely at Thy disposal,
having no will or interest of my own.
Help me to live to Thee for ever,
to make Thee my last and only end,
so that I may never more in one instance love my sinful self.

– The Valley of Vision
Page 130

PERSONAL REFLECTIONS

BIBLIOGRAPHY

Http://www.*AllAboutGod*.com/what-is-mercy-faq.htm

Boice, James Montgomery. *The Parables of Jesus*, Moody Publishers, 1983.

Biblehub.com/greek/3466.htm. *Strong's Exhaustive Concordance*, NASB Translation

Dr Benjamin L.Corey. "*10 Reasons Why People Leave Church*" http://www.patheos.com/blogs/formerlyfundie/*10-reasons-why-people-leave-church* (accessed January 2017).

Gotquestions.org/repentance.html

Kistemaker, Simon J. *The Parables*. Grand Rapids: Baker, 1980.

MacArthur, John. *Parables*; Thomas Nelson Publishing Co., Nashville, TN.

Ryrie, Ph.D, Charles Caldwell, *Ryrie Study Bible*. Moody Press, Chicago.

Scripturethoughts.wordpress.com/2011/05/21/j-c-ryle-our-talent-on-loan-from-god

Snodgrass, Klyne R. *Stories With Intent*. Wm. B. Eerdmans Publishing Co., Grand Rapids/Cambridge.

Spurgeon, Charles Haddon, "*Entrance and Exclusion*," in Metropolitan Tabernacle Pulpit, vols. 7-63 (Pasadena, Texas: Pilgrim Publications, 1976).

Strong's Exhaustive Concordance of the Bible, Nashville, TN: Abingdon Publishers, 1980, (Greek Dictionary of the New Testament).

Verbrugge, Verlyn D, *The NIV Theological Dictionary of New Testament Words,* (Zondervan Publishing House, Grand Rapids MI, 2000).

www.ingramcontent.com/pod-product-compliance
Lightning Source LLC
Chambersburg PA
CBHW080336170426
43194CB00014B/2585